MORE STORIES FOR REFLECTION

Jack McArdle ss.cc.

More
Stories for Reflection

the columba press

First published in 1997 by
the columba press
55A Spruce Avenue, Stillorgan Industrial Park,
Blackrock, Co Dublin

Cover by Bill Bolger
Origination by The Columba Press
Printed in Ireland by Colour Books Ltd, Dublin

ISBN 1 85607 202 9

Acknowledgements

I would like to acknowledge with gratitude the friends and colleagues who generously read the manuscript. Their observations have been a great help and encouragement.

Contents

	Introduction	7
1.	Salvation cannot be earned	9
2.	To know Christ	13
3.	To be Christ to others	16
4.	Heaven begins right now	20
5.	The Father stands guard	24
6.	Free at last	28
7.	Living with hope	32
8.	Total commitment	36
9.	Do it now	40
10.	Not just now	45
11.	Not everything I want	49
12.	Preparing the way ahead	53
13.	You'll find what you are	57
14.	Putting the world together	61
15.	The choice is yours	65
16.	What is happening within	69
17.	Life in abundance	73
18.	My father owns the store	77
19.	Hope, belief, or faith	81
20.	Have given you authority	85
21.	Walking with the Lord	90

22.	Knowing from experience	94
23.	Learning to listen	98
24.	Discovering the pearl within	102
25.	Bloom where you're planted	106
26.	Almost a saint	110
27.	Living in the Kingdom	114
28.	The unknown God	118
29.	Carried by the Lord	122
30.	Doing something about it	126
31.	Quality rather than quantity	130
32.	We are all sinners	134
33.	The choice is ours	138
34.	God's ways are not our ways	142
35.	Whose problem is it?	146
36.	Jesus at the door	150
37.	Me or us?	154
38.	How I see myself	158
39.	Adopted into the family	162
40.	Hunger in the midst of plenty	165
	Thematic Index	169

Introduction

In a book of mine called *Jesus: The Man and the Message,* I devoted a chapter each to many of the personal qualities displayed in the life of Jesus. He was a shepherd, a teacher, a friend, a rebel, a healer, etc. One chapter which I reluctantly omitted was *Jesus the Storyteller.* It is fascinating to see just how many stories and parables there are in the gospels. It is not unreasonable to say that this is one of his principle methods of teaching, and that his stories and parables contain the core of his message. If we wish to know his teaching and thoughts on sin, we read the stories of the Prodigal Son, the Lost Sheep, or the Pharisee and the Publican. To know his mind on love and Christian charity, we read the stories of the Good Samaritan or the Rich Man and Lazarus. To learn about prayer, we read about the Persistant Widow, or the Ten Bridesmaids. And so on and on it goes, from the Workers in the Vineyard, to the Wedding Feast, to the King, the Talents and the Servants.

Yes indeed, Jesus used stories a great deal but, most importantly, he used them well. He had a core truth to present and the stories contained that truth. Nothing about 'padding' to fill out a sermon in this! If the story was slightly complicated, he explained it and drew the message from it, as with the man who went out to sow the seed. Did he tell a story with drawings when he wrote with his finger on the ground? Was he standing right beside a vineyard when he told them about the labourers that were hired? Did he point to children playing when he told them that they refused to rejoice when he offered them happiness?

This book is a follow-up to *Stories for Reflection,* published some time ago. Once again, I have wrapped each story in a reflection, by way of teaching and of stimulating further reflection. Having done that, I can only stand back and present this book to the reader. I am presuming that different stories will help and inspire different people. It is embarrassing to listen to a story that falls flat, where even the teller seems to have missed the whole point of the story. Just as there are horses for courses, there are particular stories that appeal to particular people. It is hardly necessary to warn the preacher or teacher against using a story in speaking to others that has not already proved to be an inspiration to the speaker.

Over to you, dear reader, and may the Lord bless you through the words you read.

Jack McArdle ss cc

1. Salvation cannot be earned

Salvation is a gift from God. God doesn't give me anything: He offers me everything. When Jesus went down into the river Jordan (representing the sinners of all time), 'the heavens were opened'. When he completed that commitment on Calvary, 'the veil of the Temple was rent in two'. In other words, from that moment on, we could come into the Holy of Holies. From then on, it is possible for us to come into the presence of the all-holy God in heaven. This is something that cannot be earned. It just has to be accepted.

This can be something that religious people may find difficult to accept, because the stress of religion has always had some element of working out our salvation in it. 'Well done, thou good and faithful servant ... enter now into the joy of the Lord' surely implies a reward for a job well done. If I must insist on defining a role for myself in salvation, then I would define it as accepting the gift, because even God cannot do anything for me, without my permission. Our salvation is made up of two components, i.e. what Jesus has done, and how I accept that, and act on it. St Paul says it is 'His blood and our faith'.

Genius is the ability to discern the obvious. The problem with most things about God is that they are so basically simple that we might suspect there must be a catch somewhere! With the best intentions in the world, we can really complicate things. Jesus asked the theologians 'Who do you say that I am?', and they replied 'You are the eschatological manifestation of the ground of our being; the kerygma in which we find the ultimate meaning of our interpersonal relationships.' To which Jesus replied 'WHAT?'!! He certainly never intended being any of those things! 'Lord, you are our Moses, who has come to bring us safely through the desert of life, out of the slavery of sin and death, and into the Promised Land of the Father's eternal hug.' Salvation is gift, pure gift, and it is by the grace of God, and no other way, that we will enter heaven.

> There was a secondary school-teacher who died, and arrived at the gates of heaven. He was calmly walking in through the entrance, when Peter stopped him, and said 'Hi, hold on there! Where are you going?' 'I'm going in there', said the teacher, to which Peter replied 'Oh, no, you're not! It's not that simple. Just like you in your second-level education, we, also, have a points system in operation here.' 'Oh, I didn't know that', said the teacher. 'What is your system? How many points do I require?' 'We have set one thousand points as the requirement for entry into heaven', said Peter. 'Now, tell me something about yourself, and why you expect to get in this door.' The teacher took a deep breath, stuck out his chest (this was his big moment), and said 'I went to Mass every morning for the past forty years.' 'Very good', said Peter. 'That's one point.' The poor teacher was completely taken aback, and was nearly struck dumb when Peter asked 'And, tell me, what else did you do along the journey of life?' The teacher gathered himself together, and had another go. 'I was in the S.V.P., and in several Third World charities, and I collected a lot of money over the years.' 'How much?' asked Peter. 'Probably forty or fifty thousand pounds', said the teacher. 'Very good', said Peter. 'That's another point.' By now the poor teacher was completely deflated, and he muttered to himself, under his breath 'I'm afraid it's only by the grace of God I'm going to get in there.' Peter heard him, and he looked him straight in the eye, and said 'You are perfectly correct. It's only by the grace of God that you'll ever be able to enter those gates. If you really believe that, go right on in, because that, my friend, is the thousand points.'

I am not implying that the Masses and all the charitable works was a waste of time! Far from it. All of that could have contributed enormously to getting heaven down here, which is the vocation of the Christian. There are people around me living in hell, and my vocation is to bring heaven to them. 'Make me a channel of your peace. Where there is hatred, let me bring your love; where there is despair, let me bring your hope; where there is hunger, let me bring your bread.' I often think it is more difficult to get heaven into people than to get people into heaven! Jesus has done more than enough to get me to heaven, if I just accept the gift. As St Paul says 'It is his blood, and our faith that brings our salvation.' The only prayer Jesus taught us, the Our Father, is about life down here. It is praying that heaven might come on earth, that we might be forgiving, have what we need, rather than all we want, and that we might be protected from the evil within us, and around us. The word grace means gift, and it is literally correct to say that 'It is only by the grace of God that I will get into heaven.'

Let us look, for a moment, at our use of the past tense when we speak about Jesus, or when we quote his words. 'Lord, by your cross and resurrection you have set us free ... dying you destroyed our death, rising you restored our life ...' 'The one who eats my body and drinks my blood has everlasting life, and I will raise him up on the last day ... Your names are registered as citizens of heaven.' (In the language of today, you have a passport, a visa, and a green card for heaven). I could multiply such quotes, but, hopefully, those few will suffice to stress the fact that the work of Jesus in our salvation, is, effectively over, and now it is up to us what we are prepared to do about that. Please God, some day someone will come up with a cure for cancer. Nothing should be expected to result from that discovery, however, unless the patient is willing to accept and avail of the medicine. There is nothing automatic about God. Jesus came for the fall, as well as for the resurrection of many. He asked the man at the pool if we wanted to be healed, and he always gave the impression that, as he walked the roads of Galilee, he had the power to heal, but it only became effective when someone stopped him, and asked to be healed.

Central to the whole concept of salvation is the free gift of God's grace. In fact, there is a double emphasis there, because the word grace means gift, and, therefore, by definition, grace is always gift. I would argue strongly that we can put too much emphasis entirely on life after death. I believe salvation is available now, that heaven begins right here, and that our concern is not if there is any life after death, but how much life there is before death. When Jesus speaks of abundant life, he is speaking about something that begins now, and comes to its fruition in the third and final stage of life. The greatest thanks I could give him for all he has done for me, through his death and resurrection, is to be humble enough to gratefully and graciously accept the free gift of eternal life in his kingdom. As St John says 'to those who did receive him, he gave the gift of becoming children of God. All they had to do is to believe in his name.' And again, we are told 'there is no other name given to us in heaven or on earth, whereby we can be saved.'

Dear Jesus, thank you for dying for me. Thank you for opening the heavens again, so that I can now come right into the Holy of Holies. This is your greatest gift, a share in the divine life. Please help me, Lord, to be humble enough, and spiritual enough to accept all this for the pure free gift that it is. I console myself that, of course, I can give you something in return. I can give you great joy and happiness by my willingness to just accept the gift, and enter into the life. It was for this that you came. Thank you. Amen.

2. To know Christ

When I was growing up, we had a Christianity that was made up of rules, regulations, commandments, and definite directives to cover everything we did. We could distinguish between venial and mortal sin, right down to the last penny; we had laws, binding under sin, about what we ate on certain days, and the times when we were not permitted to eat at all. There was no end to it, as, like the Pharisees of old, we were all little moral theologians! There was no talk about love, and I was afraid of my life of God, as I made Acts of Perfect Contrition every day, in case I'd be hit by a bus, or die in my sleep!

Then came a new brand of Christianity that had my parents, and their generation, really worried! We were told about love, and we were all going to hold hands, play guitars in church, and sing songs about teaching the world to sing in perfect harmony! Now, however, there was no talk about sin, and my poor mother was wondering whatever happened to hell! The old fire and brimstone preachers were put out to grass, and no one thumped the pulpit any more!

More recently, we see another brand of Christianity, made up of Trocaire boxes, all-night vigils, charity walks, while we push beds and barrows from Dublin to Galway. We develop a Third World mentality, and we become little mini social workers. (I hasten to add that I am not against any of this! Far from it.) I do need to say, however, that Christianity is not really about any of these things. Christianity is about a person, Jesus Christ, and all those other things must follow from my commitment to him. Mother Teresa gives full credit to the social workers of the state, who work in Calcutta, but she makes a very clear distinction between their approach and hers. 'They are working for something , while we are working for Somebody.' Karl Rahner was asked, at Vatican 2 what he thought had happened to the central place of Mary in the Catholic Church, and he replied 'For many Christians, Christianity has been reduced to a set of ideals and abstractions, and abstractions don't need a mother! While Christianity is about a person, there will always be a need for a mother.'

There is a very obvious difference between a generator, that generates electricity, and the electric wire that conveys that electricity to sockets and light bulbs. Jesus is the source of our power, and we are asked to be the channels, to carry that power to others. There is a great freedom in not being responsible for providing the power. It is much easier to proclaim to people that they are saved, than to try to save them myself!

One time a group of people were discussing good and bad memories, and their retention span for things they had committed to memory. As a result of the discussion, a challenge was thrown down to anyone who would demonstrate an ability to recite something learned by heart. The first on his feet was a young lad, offering to recite Psalm 23 ('The Lord is my Shepherd') from memory. He had a clear voice, good enunciation, and some dramatic skill, as he recited the psalm in a way that drew thunderous applause at the end. In fact, on demand, he had to recite the psalm a second time, again to great applause. The second person on his feet was an elderly gentleman, who was stooped, and whose voice crackled somewhat, as he, too, recited the very same psalm. It wasn't always easy to hear him. However, the listeners soon became aware of being touched by some inner power, as each bowed a head, and felt a sense of reverent prayer rise up from the heart. The conclusion of the recital was met with complete silence, and with a sense of reverent awe. The young man who first recited the psalm was the first to respond to the situation, as he stood up and explained the different responses to the two recitals of the same psalm. He put it quite simply. 'I know the psalm', he said, 'but that old man, it is obvious that he knows the Shepherd.'

Most of us know the psalm, we have learned the definitions, we may be able to trot out all the answers. But knowing the Shepherd is not something I can ever learn from a book. There is a very great difference between academic knowledge, which is in the head, and experiential knowledge, which is in the heart. Jesus spoke of the Holy Spirit as a fountain of living water that rises up from within a person. It is of the nature of God's Spirit to begin in the heart. I could have a degree in Theology up in my head, and not really believe in God at all, down in my heart. For many years, I believed there was a huge big waterfall in Niagara, upstate New York. I visited there some years ago, and now I know, and I no longer just believe it. I could know a great deal about Jesus, but not actually know him. Jesus said 'I am the good shepherd. I know mine, and mine know me.' Jesus also speaks of the Day of Judgement, when people will say to him 'Lord, Lord, did we not speak in your name? Did we not cast out devils and perform miracles in your name?' 'Then I will say to them openly "I have never known you; away from me, you workers of evil."'

Christianity is about Incarnation, it is about Jesus making his home in us, and completing his work through us. It is about the heart, and not the head. If I speak from the heart, I speak to the heart. The nature of the Lord's presence within means that everything I do and say can be inspired by his Spirit, and, therefore, when I speak, I can expect to evoke a response within the hearts of the listeners. I fully agree with preparing a homily, or a religious knowledge lesson in a classroom, but I would see it so much more essential that I approach the task with the conviction that, unless the Spirit of the Lord is in my words, they are certainly not going to transform the hearts of any of my listeners. Jesus came to set up his kingdom among us. When Pilate asked him if he were a king, he said that that was why he came. However, it is very important for us to remember that 'the kingdom, the power, and the glory are his.' If I insist on supplying any of the power, I may easily try taking some of the glory.

Spirit of God, I know it is part of your mission on earth to reveal Jesus to us. Jesus said that you would tell us all about him, and remind us of everything he told us. I open my heart to you, with a genuine hunger and desire to come to know Jesus. To know him as my Saviour, my Lord, and my God. To know him in and through my sinfulness and brokenness. To know him as my Shepherd, who will lead me safely home. Amen.

3. To be Christ to others

Christianity is not about producing nicer people, with better morals. I could be a pagan, and be a very nice guy! It is not about prayer and fasting. I could be a Muslim, and fast for a month at a time, and pray several times a day, facing Mecca. Christianity is about Incarnation. It is about the Spirit of God coming upon us, and Jesus being formed within us, so that, as a Christian, I can say, with St Paul 'I live now, not I, but Christ lives in me.' St Paul also says that 'when a person becomes a Christian, that person becomes a brand new person inside. A new life has begun.' Christianity is about what happens inside. It is from the heart that the family resemblance with Jesus begins.

It is an accepted fact that children who are adopted into the one family develop a striking resemblance to each other as they grow up. Through my Baptism, I have been adopted into the family of God, with God as my Father, Mary as my Mother, and Jesus as my Brother. It is to be hoped that, as I struggle along the Christian way, that new family resemblance will begin to show itself more and more. With St Francis and Padre Pio, for example, the reality of Jesus living within was so evident that it showed itself in the body as well, through the marks of Jesus' wounds on hands and feet.

Christianity is about seeing Christ in others, and being Christ to others. This may seem to be a little bit idealistic, but the Spirit of God is given us to make all this possible. By ourselves, of course, we cannot do it, and it helps greatly when I accept the basic premise that I myself do not have what it takes to become a Christian, or to live as a Christian. With the Christian vocation comes the power to answer that call, and to live the Christian commitment.

It helps if I am realistic enough to accept that I never actually become a Christian, but, as G. K. Chesterton says, we are always in the process of becoming. I will never become perfect, and I will never love another as Jesus loves me. However, the direction of my life must be towards that ideal. 'Lord, I confess that I'm not as good as I ought to be, but I thank you that I am a bit better than I used to be!' God will not send me anywhere when I die. Rather will he eternalise the direction in which I now travel, and the decisions I now make. For the Christian, life can be like attending a Christian formation school all my life. I move continually from information to formation to transformation. It is a continuous process, and was represented by a little statue I saw one time. It was a man, made of modelling clay, and he had but one arm, and one leg. On the base of the statue were the words 'Please be patient with me, because God is not finished with me yet!'

> A group of men were returning from a conference, and were rushing, by taxi, to catch a train. As they arrived at the railway station, the train was ready to move off. They already had their tickets, so they rushed across the platform, and began to get on the train. In their hurry, however, one of the men accidentally brushed against a table on the platform, and scattered some of the apples that a seller had stacked neatly on display. As it happened, this man was a Christian, or at least very open to becoming one. Without further thought he shouted to the others to go ahead, and he would catch the next train. He returned to the table and the apples, to find that the person in charge was a twelve-year-old boy, and he was blind. He was waiting on his mother to return from a shop across the road. The man gathered the scattered apples, put aside some that were slightly damaged, and stacked the others neatly, just as they had been before he hit the table. When the job was finished, the man took some money from his pocket, put it in the boy's hand, and said 'That will cover the apples that are damaged. I'm sorry for what has happened, and I hope I haven't spoiled your day.' He squeezed the boy's hand in a reassuring way, and turned to walk away. As he did so, the boy, who was blind, turned in his direction, and asked simply 'Excuse me sir, but … eh … eh … are you Jesus?'

And that is exactly what we are to be towards others. As I've said before, the ideal of Christianity is to see Christ in others, and to be Christ to others. I readily admit that it's often impossible to see

Christ in others, but I would suggest that it becomes so much easier to do so when I begin to be Christ to others. If I could see Christ in them first, there would be little credit in my treating them with love and kindness. However, I am suggesting that when I begin to treat others with love and kindness, I will discover a very different person there than the one I first encountered. How often we hear it said 'She's really very nice when you get to know her'!

The symbol of Christianity is the cross, formed by the vertical and the horizontal. The vertical represents God and me, while the horizontal represents me and others. The ideal is to strive for a balance between the two. God does not want to hear me say to him 'I love you, I thank you, I praise you, or I'm sorry', unless the people in my life hear that first. What comes from God to me must go sideways to others; otherwise it ceases to come from God. If forgiveness does not go sideways from me to others, it ceases to come from God to me. I do not advise it or advocate it, but if you want to know how much you love God, then look sideways, and ask yourself: who is the person in your life that you love least? That's how much you love me, says Jesus. 'Whatsoever you do to the least of these, that's what you do onto me.'

In Matthew 25 we are given the questions that will be asked on the last day. I remember coming across a version one time that went something like this: 'I was hungry, and you told me that you would build war machines to make me secure. I was thirsty, and you told me that the world's resources were already stretched to their limits, and it was time to get rid of the excess population. I was a stranger, and you banded together, because you said you could trust only your own kind. I was naked, and you told me that the poor will always be with us. I was ill, and you said you were tired of misfits always complaining about the way things are. I was in prison, and you told me that charity begins at home. The problem with Christianity is that Christians want to be committed to Christ, without being committed to Christ's brothers and sisters. Mahatma Ghandi was employed doing menial work in London during his earlier years. Someone gave him a copy of the Gospels to read. When he had finished reading, he remarked that, after reading the Gospels, he had come to admire Christ, but to despise the so-called Christianity being practiced around him.

Lord Jesus, there are times when you fill me with wonder! You came to take my place, and you ended up arranging that I could take your place! I can actually be your ambassador in the lives of others. Oh, Lord, if it were not for the presence and power of your Spirit, I couldn't dare even to consider such a thing. Thank you for the privilege, and for the grace that makes it all possible. Thank you, Lord. Amen.

4. Heaven begins right now

The road to heaven is heaven, and the road to hell is hell. People with a worldly mind-set, who do not get in touch with their hearts, might think that the road to heaven is hell, and the road to hell is heaven! (Think about it!) I believe that there is nothing I get when I die that I am not offered now. God does not give me anything, he offers me everything. Jesus said he would not leave us orphans, and then he offers us his Father and his mother, and he tells us that it will only work if we become like little children.

Selfishness is a form of loneliness, and total selfishness is a form of solitary confinement, where there is no one but myself in my life. The more people I open my heart to, the richer my life becomes. Mr Scrooge, in Charles Dickens' 'The Christmas Carol', is a very good example of the hell we can create for ourselves through selfishness and miserliness. It is one of the central paradoxes of Christianity that 'it is in giving that we receive'. Let me suggest a thought here. Supposing I waken up on Monday morning feeling on top of the world. I have a great sense of peace and contentment. By ten o'clock I meet someone who is really down in the dumps, and I do not attempt to share with that person what I myself have. I would not be surprised if, by eleven o'clock, my own peace was gone! If, on the other hand, I share what I have, it is very possible that, by eleven o'clock, I will have even a greater peace and sense of well-being. In other words, I am suggesting that God doesn't give me anything for myself. (He doesn't give me my gift of speech to go around talking to myself!)

Let me throw in an extra story here, which may amuse, but, more importantly, may make a very important point about how we can become locked up in our little worlds, to the exclusion of others. A woman went into a supermarket, bought her groceries, and went into a coffee shop in the mall, to treat herself to a coffee and a kit-kat. She put her bags of groceries on the ground, and began to sip her coffee. The man sitting opposite her reached over, picked up the kit-kat bar, broke off a piece, and put it in his mouth. The woman was highly indignant, but she said nothing, as she grabbed the kit-kat, broke off a large chunk, and began to eat it. The man took another section of the kit-kat, which really infuriated her, as she grabbed the remaining piece, and shoved it into her mouth. At that, the man got up, went over to the counter, where he bought himself another cup of coffee, and a scone, and proceeded to a table in the corner. The woman was beside herself with anger at this stage, especially as he was so cool and laid-back about the whole thing. She picked up her groceries, and, as she passed his table, she picked up his scone, took a huge bite out of it, put it back on his plate, with the one word 'There'. She headed on out to the car park, quite happy with herself, and the stand she took. As she was putting her bags of groceries in the car, she went weak with the shock of realisation, as she saw there, on the top of one of her bags was her kit-kat!! (It is generally believed that she hasn't appeared in that shopping centre since!)

There once was a man who was very curious to know what heaven and hell might look like. One night he had a dream, and he was taken off to visit heaven and hell. He visited hell first. He was amazed to find that hell consisted of a large room, with a long table down the centre, and the table was laden down with every possible variety of the most beautiful and delicious food. The people who sat around the table, however, were in complete frustration and misery, and were dying of hunger. The reason for this was that they all had two five-foot-long chopsticks, and were just not able to get the food in their mouths.

The man was then taken to visit heaven. He was even more surprised to see that heaven also consisted of a large room, with a long table down the centre. Once again, the table was laden down with delicious food, and the people here also sat around the table, each with two five-foot-long chopsticks. There was one vast difference here from the other room. The people were completely happy and healthy, as each picked up food with the chopsticks, and reached out to feed the person sitting opposite!

This story speaks for itself, of course, but I would like to add a short reflection. On occasions, through the life of a relative or acquaintance who is an alcoholic, for example, we see the results of self-will run riot. There seems to be some sort of crazy insanity, that is hell-bent on self-destruction, and then to the destruction of anyone else who becomes involved.

Jesus said that he came that we might have life, and have it more abundantly. To be a life-giving person, I must have a sense of service. This has nothing whatever to do with grovelling subordination, or being a door-mat for anyone. It is simply to acknowledge that no one is an island; we are all part of the mainland, and we do have an obligation to each other. 'Am I my brother's keeper?' is a question that was asked many many years ago, and the answer still is 'Yes, you are; in so far as whatever you do for the least of these, I will take as being done for me.'

Just as I can mediate life to another, so I can mediate death. That is a frightening thought. Really selfish people are to be pitied, because such people do not know what they are missing, and what they deprive themselves of..There is a marvellous statement in the Letter to the Hebrews 'Keep your eyes fixed on Jesus, the author and finisher of our faith, who, because of the joy that lay in the future, willingly submitted to die on a cross, scorning its shame, and now he sits at the right hand of the throne of God.' Right there we have a whole way of thinking and living. Scott Peck would call it 'delaying gratification', where we face up to some unpleasant action or decision now, knowing that it will be followed by the satisfaction that comes from doing the right thing, and from doing things correctly. For example, it is a miserable day outside, and I know I should travel across town to visit someone in hospital. As I think about it, it is the last thing I feel like doing right now. However, I act on my decision, for the sake of another, and, as I go towards my car in the parking lot, after having visited the hospital, I know the good feeling that comes from doing the right thing. In miniature, it is a little of Easter, following on a little of Good Friday. There is nothing more powerful than an idea whose Time has come. The short-term pain for the long-term gain. Happy are they who dream dreams, and are prepared to pay the price to make their dreams come through. It is not enough to talk the talk. I must be ready and willing to walk the walk.

Lord Jesus, I thank you that you have made it very clear to us what heaven is all about. You brought heaven down here when you touched the leper, hugged the children, and fed the hungry. I pray that your Spirit may continue to call me out of myself, towards others, to be a person for others, to bring heaven to others, and so, to live in heaven myself, right here, right now. Amen.

5. The Father stands guard

Life is a journey, a journey of faith. It is a continuous learning process. From the moment of birth the instincts of the baby are cultivated and guided, through breast-feeding, bottle-feeding, holding some object, or learning to make various sounds. Right from the start, it is obvious that this learning process is based, primarily, on success, failure, and starting again. I hesitate to use the word 'failure' here, because, by the nature of things, there is no such thing as failure at this early stage. Take, for example, the whole walking process. This is developed through taking a step, falling backwards, hitting a head on the leg of a chair, reverting to crawling, etc. And then, here we go again, and the whole process begins all over again. If you were to make a video of this from that first faltering step until the child is running around the place, and every time the baby falls and gets it wrong, you pause the video to study the incident, you would surely have to agree that there was no failure along the way. You would accept, I hope, that such falls were a necessary part of the process of learning to walk. Success here is measured, not by never falling, but by getting up every time we fall.

The journey of faith is somewhat similar to that journey towards walking. If I exercise the gift of faith I have, if I continue to practice the gift, my ability to trust will grow. There is one very important point here that must be stressed. Education comes from the Latin 'educare', which means 'to bring out'. It involves discovering and bringing out the gifts and talents the person possesses. I cannot put in a gift or a talent. If the child does not have a talent for music or for art, I can put that child through a veritable hell, insisting that he/she continue attending classes, to develop a talent the child does not possess. Given that the child has normal limb and muscle function, it is right to expect the child to use these, and so develop the ability to walk. Because of our Baptism, we do have the gift of

24

faith, but, once again, this gift must be exercised, or it will not be developed.

Faith is a response to love. Please don't ask me to trust someone until you have first convinced me that this person cares about me, and has my interests at heart. Faith eventually ends up down in my feet, when I am ready to step out in confidence. Some people can confuse faith with knowledge. Up in my head, I know that Jesus is God. That is only knowledge, and I must remember that even Satan knows that Jesus is God! How I am prepared and willing to respond to such knowledge is the acid test of my faith.

There was a young lad, a member of an Indian tribe, who was taken out into the jungle, on the eve of his thirteenth birthday. The idea was that he should spend the night there alone, as a test of his courage, and his suitability for acceptance into young manhood in the tribe.

The night was very long. It was his first experience of being alone in such an unfriendly environment. Every sound seemed to be amplified by the surrounding silence. Every movement in the under-growth, every branch that creaked, every leaf that fell, sent a shiver up his spine. There was no way he could sleep. What made it worse, there was no way he could run away, because it was so dark; and, anyhow, he could not risk going further and further into the jungle.

He hit many a pocket of despair, as he waited and longed for the dawn. He never knew that a night could be so long. Anyhow, eventually, after what seemed like ages, the dawn began to filter through the trees. Soon his eyes became used to the growing light, and he was able to look around him, and to distinguish the trees from the bushes, and the briars from the grass. As he looked around, he thought he saw some movement behind one of the trees, and, as he approached very carefully, he was amazed to see his father standing there, with a hunting rifle in his hand. Apparently, he had been standing there all night, watching over his son, lest any of the wild creatures of the jungle attack him. The son's reaction was immediate, as he thought to himself: 'If I had known that my dad was watching over me like that, I would have slept soundly all night.'

The whole gospel could be summarised in one sentence: The Father loves me. If I died this moment, I could well be asked by Jesus: 'Did you really come to believe that my Father loved you?' If I expressed any surprise at the question, Jesus could well say 'But that's why I came. I told you that your heavenly Father knows your needs, and he is continually looking over you, and looking out for your needs.'

In the one prayer that Jesus taught us, he told us to ask for our daily bread, just enough for today. That is the secret of getting to know the Father's love and care. Each morning I waken up, I am given a whole new day, and, written all over the gift are the words 'batteries included'. Lord, help me to believe that nothing is going to happen today that you and I, together, will not be able to handle. It is only when I slow life down to segments that I have any hope of coming to grips with its secrets. God is totally a God of now ... 'I am who am' ... and if I could ever become a person of now, I would come face to face with God.

This concept of the Father's love is so central to the whole Christian message that I do not need to apologise for repetition on this subject. It cannot be sufficiently or adequately stressed. At the Last Supper, Jesus prayed that 'they may know, Father, that you love them as much as you love me.' Jesus' whole life was the equivalent of going into the jungle for over thirty years, and knowing that the Father was standing guard. Everything Jesus tells us about the Father is reinforcing this simple message. He himself lived the message, and then he taught it to those who had seen it in practice. He announced that he never said anything unless the Father told him to say it. He then went on to tell the story of the Prodigal Son, and the forgiving father, which is the gospel message in summary. He spoke of the birds of the air, and the lilies of the field, and how his Father was concerned for all of these. 'How much more will he care for you, oh you of little faith.' He even said that, as far as his Father was concerned, the very hairs of our heads are numbered. In other words, in the words of the Psalmist, God knows me through and through. He knows all about me, and he plots the path ahead of me.

It is very important that I accept the simple fact that flesh and blood can never reveal this to me. This is primarily the work of the Holy Spirit, who leads into all truth. The greatest truth of all has to do with the love of God the Father for all his children. Jesus said he would not leave us orphans. He then went on to offer us his Father and his mother. He warned us, however, that it would only work if we were prepared to become like little children.

In a way, life can be compared to a night in a dark jungle, except, as a Christian, I should know that my Father is standing guard over every breath I breathe. I expect this to be definitely confirmed, following the moment of death, when I am free of the body, and the limitations that such a condition imposes. I will see clearly then how my Father had held me in the palm of his hand, and how everything He allowed happen to me had a potential for good, whether I accepted that or not. The saint is someone who believes that now, and who does not need to die to get the proof, before believing. The atheist would believe if the proof could be given first. There would be no virtue in that. Jesus asks me to believe him now, and then I can spend my eternity marvelling at the proof.

Heavenly Father, I know that when I die, I will discover just how much you loved me during life, and how well you cared for me. Please help me, through your Spirit, not to wait for the proof, but to accept the fact of your love now. You have carved me on the palm of your hand, and I rest safely in your loving care. I thank you. Amen.

6. Free at last

Without wishing to be too philosophical, it could help if I had a clear idea of just what I am. Am I a physical being, with a spiritual dimension? If so, I will live with that emphasis, giving priority to the physical, and treating the spiritual as some sort of appendage. If, on the other hand, I accept that I am a spiritual being, living in a physical dimension; and, if I go further, and accept the fact that I'm living in this physical dimension for a relatively short time, then that should profoundly effect things. When Scripture speaks of the connection between prayer and fasting, I think of this as being an attempt to correct an imbalance. Fasting helps to discipline the body, and prevents the body dictating the actions of the person. On the other hand, prayer boosts the spirit, and gives a greater inner strength, that enables a person be more faithful to the authentic inspirations of the inner being. The body is the product of a human act, while the inner spirit is created directly by God, and is made in his image and likeness.

The body is not me. I am living in the body for just so long. When that time is up, I'll go on to the third and final stage of life, and leave the body behind, ... which explains why the body at that stage is often called the 'remains'. I myself carry an organ-donor card, allowing the use of any parts that may be useful, after I've finished with them. (Incidentally, I discovered recently that, after my fiftieth birthday, the powers-that-be in the transplant field don't, literally, want any part of me!) I will never go into a coffin. By the time my body is placed in a coffin, I, that inner real me, will have gone ahead to the third and final stage of life. By then I will have come through the womb life, and the womb of life, and will have become what God created me to be, in the first place. I'm sure this thought will come at you several times during these reflections, but here it is again: If you ever waken up some morning, and your life is the way it should be, please don't move! Just remain as you are, and wait for the undertaker! You have arrived!

A lady is preparing to leave home in the morning to go to work. Her job is an important one, she is in the public eye, and her appearance is something to which she must pay special attention. She goes through her regular morning routine with great attention, and, before going out the door, she checks her appearance in the mirror one last time. She is satisfied with what she sees, as she remarks 'Now I'm ready to face the new day.' Just then she was very conscious of a tiny inner voice that said 'Your outer person is ready, but what about your inner person? You've had breakfast for your body, but have you nourished your spirit and your soul? Just how ready is the real you to face this new day? How much resentment, unforgiveness, guilt, do you bring into this new day, – something that may well spill over on those around you, as the day goes on?'

One of the most positive aspects of Christianity is its teaching about death, and the very important relationship there is between the outer person (body) and the inner (soul/spirit).

There was a little girl out for a walk with her dad, and they were strolling through the local cemetery. After a while, the child pointed to the graves, and the tomb-stones, and asked 'Daddy, what are those?' The dad was caught off guard for a moment, as he struggled to find a simple and suitable answer. 'Eh, these were people who lived in those houses down there one time, and then Holy God sent for them to come to live in his house, with all his angels.' She thought about that for a few moments, and then, as happens with that age-group, another question follows 'And, daddy, did they go off to live in Holy God's house, with all his angels?' The dad, with fingers crossed, replied 'Yes, they did.' She thought about that for a while, and then her face lit up with a look of understanding, as she said 'And daddy, guess what? I bet you when they went off to live in Holy God's house with all his angels, this is where they left their clothes.'

And she was right! The body is like the rockets on a space shuttle, which, when they have given direction and propulsion to the shuttle, are then discarded, and fall back to earth. When the body has served its purpose, it then returns to earth, and to clay, from which it came.

What, then, of 'the resurrection of the body' on the last day? It is our belief that the bodies we have now do not have the necessary qualities for eternal living, and, while we will have actual bodies for eternity, those bodies will be transformed copies of the bodies we now possess. St Paul writes 'Our earthly bodies which die and decay, are different from the bodies we shall have when we come back to life again, for they will never die. The bodies we now have embarrass us, for they become sick and die; but they will be full of glory when we come back to life again. Yes, they are weak, dying bodies now, but when we live again they will be full of strength.' (1 Cor 15:42-43).

After his resurrection, Jesus' body was glorified, capable of passing through the walls of the room in which the apostles were gathered. On the other hand, he went to great lengths to convince them that his body was real. He invited them to touch him, to give him something to eat; while he himself actually prepared a meal for them. On the morning of the resurrection, when the women arrived at the tomb, an angel told them that, if they were looking for Jesus, he was not there, but he invited them to look inside and see 'where he had left his clothes'. The clothes in question were actually the cloths in which his body was wrapped for burial. When Jesus raised Lazarus from the dead, he asked the people gathered there 'to unbind him, and set him free'. In other words, Lazarus would have smothered and died again, because of being bandaged from head to foot. Jesus raised him from the dead, but it was now up to the community to 'set him free'. The idea of my community assisting my emergence into freedom, is a dimension of Christian living that may not be sufficiently stressed. In his own case, this was all done without human help or assistance. The work of redemption, the victory over sin, sickness, and death, was something that God alone would do, and that God alone could do.

I myself believe it is very important, at a funeral, to understand exactly what is going on. The deceased person is not in the coffin, but has now passed on into the third and final stage of life. The person hasn't gone *away*, but has simply gone *ahead*. The body, up till now, has been a temple of God's divine in-dwelling, and will be raised in a glorified condition, capable of living for eternity. Therefore, we show great respect for the body, in the funeral services. We use holy water, incense, etc., and, in the case of a burial, we respectfully bring the body to be placed in consecrated ground. In a way, just as the church is people, whether they are in a building, or out in the open, so do we respect the buildings in which God's church meets for worship, and hence the respect that we have traditionally had for such places of worship. They become sacred through the functions they serve, just as the body is given a reverence because of the purpose it has served. At the time of a funeral, however, it can help to make a clear distinction between burying a body, and remembering a person. For the time being, until the general resurrection, this, in the words of the little girl, 'is where they leave their clothes when they go home to live in Holy God's house with all his angels'.

Lord Jesus, I thank you for overcoming the three evils of sin, sickness, and death. I believe and accept this, even if I don't fully understand it. When I leave the body, I want to do so with total trust in your love. I ask for the grace to take this step willingly and with confidence. Lord, after all this time, and after all you have done for me, if I cannot trust you, who can I ever trust? Thanks, Lord, in advance, for being there. I leave the part about the return of the body totally up to you! Thanks, Lord. Amen.

7. Living with hope

I often joke about meeting and knowing some people who will find something to complain about in heaven! They are people who badly need an optical adjustment to their view of life, so that they see more than the negative and the problem-side. 'Two men looked out through their prison bars. One saw the mud on the road, the other, the beauty of the stars.' I'm sure most of us have been faced with a sheet of white paper, with a small ink stain on it, and asked 'What do you see?' The expected, and the normal answer is 'An ink stain' or 'A black spot'. The correct answer, of course, is 'I see a white page, 99.9% white, with a small black mark on it.' And then, of course, we have the classic debate about whether the beer glass is half-empty or half-full! For those to whom I refer at the beginning of this paragraph, the glass is definitely half-empty! The summer just ended was one of many and wonderful sunny days. I remember, on one of the first good days, remarking about the beautiful weather, to be told, with foreboding 'Oh, we'll pay for this before the summer is out!' What a pity that such people see hidden price tags on all gifts, even the pure gifts given by God!

I believe that it makes basic common sense to accept and appreciate my strengths, before I can hope to deal with my weaknesses. It is a question of where I begin. Do I begin with my sins, or do I begin with God's love and acceptance of me? I believe that when I make myself my starting point, I am on the path to discouragement and pessimism. There is a sentence in Scripture that I particularly like 'Keep your eyes fixed on Jesus, the author and founder of our faith … For the sake of the joy that lay in the future, he endured the cross' (Heb 12:2). By keeping my mind on the positive, the reward, I can endure the pain. It's the short-term pain for the long-term gain. Take, for example, someone on a diet to lose weight. It can be tough going, and the effort can prove too much. If, however, that person has a lovely new suit, about two sizes too small, hanging where it can be seen every day; and is aware of a great longing to wear that suit some day, ... that positive view-point can counter-act the negativity of discouragement.

What is most important in the learning process for children is caught, and not taught. Any child can be formed to be an optimist or a pessimist. I cannot renew people. I can renew the atmosphere in which they live and breathe, and they will become renewed. A parish that strives to develop a Christian atmosphere, will produce a Christian community. On the other hand, I cannot corrupt people. I can, however, corrupt the atmosphere in which people work, and the rest will follow. Parents have a great burden of responsibility in the attitudes they instill in their children. In the home, and in the school, the children are not being prepared for life, because their lives have started years ago! It's an old adage in education to say 'Give me a child till he's four, and you can do whatever you want with him after that.'

> One time there were two little lads, one of whom was a pessimist, and the other an optimist. The pessimist was always 'whinging' about something, while the optimist, although badly defeated at games today, was determined that he was going to win tomorrow. The pessimist was put into a room that was full of toys of every description, while the optimist was put into a room full of manure from the farmyard.

> One hour later they were checked on. The pessimist, in the room full of toys, was seated on the floor in the middle of the toys, and he was crying. When asked the reason for this, he replied that he was crying because there was no drum! They then checked on the optimist in the room full of manure from the farmyard. When they opened the door, he didn't notice them, because he was so busy, with a little shovel, as he shovelled the manure from one side of the room to the other. When asked why he did this, he turned to them with eyes filled with excitement, and whispered with total conviction 'With all this manure, there's just got to be a pony here somewhere'!

One of the marks of a Christian is to be, literally, an eternal optimist! 'All things work together for good, for those who love God' (Rom 8:28). The only real sin for a Christian is to lose hope. I can safely hazard a guess that this phrase is repeated throughout this book more than any other one. That's how important I think it is. When I say that God can turn everything into good, I mean that exactly. On the human level, the Garden was a disaster, and, yet, St Augustine could say with total conviction 'Oh happy fault, that merited so great a Redeemer'. Similarly, on a human level, Calvary was a disaster, and yet the Father accepted what happened there, and used it for the salvation of the world. I sometimes think of this as Satan shooting himself in the foot, or planting a bomb that blew up in his face. The only value the past has are the lessons it taught me. Even my sins from the past can help make me a much better person today. Because of them, I can be so much more empathetic, and less ready to judge and condemn others. I can have a much deeper appreciation of God's love, and be more convinced of my own brokenness and limitations.

When I die I will see that everything that happened to me in life had a potential for good, whether I availed of it or not, or whether I saw it as such, or not. Someone like St Francis of Assisi, for example, didn't wait till he died to acknowledge that fact. That is why if today was good, he thanked and praised God, and if today was going all wrong he also thanked and praised God. Convinced that he would get all possible proof in heaven later on, he acted on that conviction now. The atheist would want and demand the proof first! A prayer worth reflecting on would be 'Lord, help me believe that everything you permit happen to me in life is seen by you as necessary for my spiritual growth'. That would surely be the prayer of the optimist!

The above story of the pessimist and optimist is worth some reflection, because such people actually exist, and, in fact, they co-exist in the same world! Some believe this world to be the worst of all possible places, while others believe we are living in the best of all possible worlds. Fundamental to the Christian message is that evil can never triumph, even if seen to be successful for a while. That is the final message of Jesus before he returned to the Father. He has overcome the world, and all the evils thereof. Of course, I won't have everything (no drum!), but I sure have a destiny, and I have a God of love who guarantees that destiny. I may have to do my share of shovelling at times, but I can be sure and certain that there are blessings in abundance awaiting the searcher, and those who push ahead with hope.

> *Lord Jesus, I really do want to trust you so totally that I just know you are present in every situation. I look to you, and to you only, to keep me from despair. I have no reason to trust myself, but I sure have every reason under heaven to trust you. Even in the toughest struggle, I pray for the grace of knowing, and of remembering something that, somewhere within my being, I now accept as true: You are there, and you are much better than any pony! Thanks, Lord. Amen.*

8. Total commitment

There are as many ways of giving as there are givers. Some give with one hand, and take back with the other. Some give till it hurts, while others give till it's gone. God loves a cheerful giver, we are told, and we are also told that it is in giving that we ourselves receive.

Faith is a response to love. The more convinced I am of God's love, the more generous my response to that love will be. While conceding that the human mind is away out of its depth in trying to explore and understand the scope and extent of God's love, it is important that I open my heart to the fulness of that love, so that, in time, my own response might be as generous as is possible for me. There's no way I can repay God's love for me, and there is no way I can be expected to repay it. That is, if I speak of depth and scope. The reality, however, is that I can meet God's 100% love with a genuine desire that he should have my 100% love, and, even if those loves are an infinity apart, they are totally balanced in the eyes of God. I can never quantify anything like this, on my side. Is it 70%, 50%, 90%. I cannot know, so I tell God that I want to give the 100%, and I ask him to come and get it!

I remember reading a book many years ago entitled 'The man who got even with God'. He was a gangster, who was eaten up with a burning desire to get even with everyone who had ever wronged him. He was converted to the Gospel message, and he entered a monastery of enclosed monks. His whole approach, from a totally different point of view, and with a totally different approach, was to get even with God. God had given him everything, so he was determined to get even with God by giving God everything he was and had. I am more than convinced that my openness and commit-- ment to God is directly in proportion to how I see God dealing with me. Saints such as Thérèse of Lisieux, or Francis of Assisi, for example, were on fire with the love of God, because His love for them was so evident and tangible that their hearts burned within them.

A chicken and a pig were out for a walk. The pig was not too bright or original, and tended to repeat what others said. The chicken said 'They're very good people down in that farmhouse.' 'They are, indeed,' said the pig. 'They're very good people.' 'They're very good to us,' continued the chicken. 'They are, indeed, they're very good to us', repeated the pig. 'Do you know what I was thinking?' asked the chicken. 'No, what were you thinking? replied the pig. 'I think we should do something for them.' 'That's a very good idea. I agree. I think we should do something for them. What did you have in mind?' 'I was thinking we should give them something.' 'A very good idea' replied the pig. 'I think we should give them something. What did you have in mind?' 'I was thinking we should give them bacon and eggs.' The pig stopped in his tracks, lifted his snout in the air, and declared with firmness 'No way! For you that's only a little inconvenience, but for me it's a total commitment!'

Jesus said that we are either for him, or against him. In the last book of the Bible (Revelations) there's a very strong word from God on lukewarmness. 'I wish that you were hot or cold. But because you are lukewarm, I will begin to vomit you out of my mouth.'(Rev 3:15) In simple English, this is saying 'you make me sick!' Surely a strong word from God! God is love, total, unconditional, pure love. The word 'love' can be so trivialised in song and story that it can lose its impact as something truly extraordinary. Love is about giving. It is about gifts, and gifts are items without price tags.

Jesus speaks of the greatest love as laying down one's life for another. Without abusing the meaning of that concept, I would not confine it to some once-off dying for another. In that case, I would only have one life to give, and, therefore, only one person to really love! I would suggest that every time I put another person in front of myself, I am dying to myself for the sake of another, and, therefore, am close to the highest form of love. I can very well ask myself when was the last time I died for someone else? That was the last time I really loved another.

The cross on Calvary was not intended for Jesus. It had been prepared for Barabbas, and he would have died on it, had not Jesus
taken his place, so that Barabbas could walk free. In more recent
times we know the story of Saint Maximilian Kolbe. A man in the
concentration camp had been condemned to death. He was a young
man with a family. Maximilian was a Franciscan priest. He stepped
forward, and offered to take the man's place, and his offer was
accepted. The man went free, and some years back he was to be
seen on our television screens, as he wept tears of appreciation and
gratitude at the canonisation of the saint in Rome.

Yes, love is about more than a little inconvenience. It is about a commitment, a personal acceptance of responsibility for the welfare of
another. If there could be any such thing as the ideal personality, it
would include the following three qualities: genuineness, empathy,
and unpossessive love. That last one can be difficult, because of the
nature we possess as humans. It is part of our damaged nature, due
to original sin, that, of ourselves, we cannot rise above our own
immediate interests, or our own personal concerns. Anything outside that requires inspiration, and sometimes perspiration. Our
most basic instinct is self-preservation. It is not natural for us to be
comfortable with dying, because every instinct within us causes us
to cling to life, and to all that benefits us in life. On a certain level,
and with certain people, love is accompanied by a feeling of love.
Love, however, is a decision. I cannot control or 'manage' feelings,
but I can control decisions. Animals act on feelings and instincts,
while humans are called to act on decisions and choices.

Religion can be about obligations, about qualified and quantified
endeavour. I don't think that God is too interested in the number of
prayers we say. He is more interested in the depth than the length
of our prayers. I can be at Mass because it is a Sunday, and there is
nothing more involved in my presence than the incidental fact that
it happens to be a certain day of the week. I can go through the
motions, like the bishop who dreamt he was preaching a sermon,
and he woke up to discover that he was! On the other hand, I can be
at Mass, and be genuinely delighted to be there, and I am there
because of a deliberate decision, and this might have nothing to do
with what day of the week it is. I can open my mouth to receive
Communion, because that is how Communion is received, or I can

open my heart, and my whole being, and receive Jesus on my tongue, so that he can enter my heart. Commitment is more about attitude than mathematics. There is a vast difference between a contract and a covenant. I can go into a shop, pay a certain sum of money, walk back out with the item, and the contract is over. We don't owe each other anything. A covenant, on the other hand, is something that is on-going. I can break a contract, but a covenant is something that cannot be broken. Scripture uses the word covenant to describe our relationship with God. Like marriage vows, it is intended that all of this will be brought to permanent consummation. As I said love is about giving. Now I add that love is about giving all that I am. It is about giving till it hurts, and about giving till it's gone. This is the everyday dying that is the call of the Christian.

If I ever come to appreciate God's unconditional love for me (and I'm not sure this is possible to a mere human), I will begin the journey towards total commitment. I will never become a Christian, I will never be able to make a total commitment to God, or to anyone else. Only God is perfect, and I am not expected to be anything other than who and what I am. God does not make demands. He promises 'peace on earth to those of good-will'. All I can hope to offer is my good-will and my availability, and I can trust the good Lord to do the rest. As at Cana, I can supply the water, and await the miracle. With Mary, I can say 'O.K. Lord. Take over. Fire away. Do with me what you wish.' That is as much of a total commitment as I can ever hope to make. I leave the rest to Him ...

Lord Jesus, I have no reason to think that I could ever make a total commitment to anything! Oh, I am sometimes aware of the good-will to do so, but my track record is not all that impressive. However, Lord, I console myself with the thought that I genuinely would love to let you have all that I have, and all that I am. I just have to believe that that's a start! I know it is your Spirit who began this, so I just have to trust your Spirit to bring this to completion. Thanks, Lord. Amen.

9. Do it now

The only real moment of time is now. Yesterday went away at midnight, and will never return. Tomorrow is very unstable currency. If I could really become a person of now, I would begin to fully live the life God has entrusted to me. Today is the day for doing all those things I'm always going to do some other time! Procrastination is the thief of time, and one of the ways of never getting around to doing anything is to continue discussing it, or thinking about it.

The road to hell is paved with good intentions. I could come to the end of my life, and discover that I almost did something worthwhile, but never actually got around to it! Life is a gift, given by God, to be used in the service of others. It is in giving that I receive. A life that is spent, is a life that is given away for the sake of others. Jesus tells us that if we strive to save our lives, we risk losing them. He tells the story of the talents, which is basically about using or not using the gifts given us. I will be held responsible for every gift God has given me, because he gives me nothing for myself.

Let us consider a little scenario for a moment. There is a car accident, where the car goes out of control, mounts the footpath, and kills one of two pedestrians who just happen to be passing by. I don't pretend to understand this, but I can well surmise that the person who wasn't killed is left with the responsibility of living out the remainder of life for the sake of others, and, who knows, but there just may be a definite reason why such a person was spared. I cannot accept that I can claim the privileges of life without assuming the responsibilities. I remember speaking with a young woman in her twenties who was dying of cancer. I was getting her to share what was going on in her, so that she could acknowledge any angers, fears, or worries she had. She made one statement that I have often considered, 'I was thinking only today that I would much prefer to die young, having fully lived those years, than to live into old age, and never have done anything with my life.'

In a way, life is an end in itself. It is not so much a journey towards something, as a journey into something. Pity those people who spend their lives saving money, to be surrounded on their death-bed by those who are all-too-ready to spend it! The road to heaven is heaven, just as the road to hell is hell.

A cow and a pig were out for a walk one day. The pig was very depressed, and the cow enquired what it was that bothered him. He admitted to being very discouraged, and very pessimistic about life, and about his place in the unfolding of events. When pressed for details, he spoke of the way he was used as a symbol for insult and infamy. Last week he heard a mother say that her son's bedroom was like a pig-sty. He heard of someone who snores like a pig, and another who eats like a pig. At no time did he hear any reference to him being used in a laudatory way. 'It's alright for you,' he told the cow. 'People don't use language like that when they speak of you. They use very polite language like 'milking parlour', for example.' 'But surely,' said the cow, 'you know the reason for the different way of speaking about us both?' 'No, I don't,' replied the pig. 'What's the reason?' 'Look at all I give them,' said the cow. 'I give them milk, butter, cream, and cheese.' 'But what about me?' retorted the pig, with annoy-ance. 'Look at all I give them. I give them bacon, ham, pork, and sausages.' 'Ah, but there's a very big difference in the giving,' replied the cow. 'I give it to them while I'm still alive! In your case they have to kill you to get anything from you!'

I shall pass this way but once. Any good deed that I can do, any good word that I can say, let me do it now, let me say it now, because I will never pass this way again. People of my generation grew up with a religion that stressed doing all possible to ensure getting to heaven after death. Life was an opportunity to collect Brownie points, and the hope was, that, when the day of reckoning came, the tally would be sufficient. I honestly do not accept that today. When I enter the eternal bliss of heaven, I will see clearly, beyond all possible doubt, that this is pure and simple gift, and I have received it because Jesus died to earn it for me. I would strongly

contend that my vocation, as a Christian, has more to do with getting heaven down here, while I am alive, than getting to heaven
myself after I die. It is much more difficult to get heaven into people
than to get people into heaven!

There may be people all around me who are living in a virtual hell.
Make me a channel of your peace. Where there is hatred, let me sow
your love. Where there is despair, let me bring your hope; where
there is hunger, let me bring your food. My vocation is to be an
instrument of God's love, mercy, and compassion to those around
me. After receiving Jesus in Communion, I can pray 'Lord, may
your presence within me touch the lives of those I meet today,
either through the words I say, the prayers I pray, the life I live, or
the very person I am.' I hear the words 'I stand at the door and
knock.' So I open my heart, and invite Jesus to make his home in
me. Later, during the day, I hear a knock at the door of my heart,
and, if I enquire what that is about, I am told 'I want back out again!
I came to you so that you could bring me to others. You are my
touch-person in the lives of others.' I have said already that God
gives me nothing for myself. Jesus comes to me so that He can go
back out to others through my words and actions.

When I reflect on the gospels, I realise that they begin with the invitation to 'Come and see', and end with the command to 'Go and
tell.' The more I come and see, the more I have to go and tell, and
the more I will have to tell when I go. I cannot speak with any conviction about salvation, forgiveness, or love, unless I myself have a
deep personal experience of such in my own life. I honestly believe
that a stress on getting to heaven myself after I die, can be a pathetic
ego-trip, where I am the centre of my own world. Could EGO stand
for Edging God Out?! I read a book some time ago, by Edward
Farrell, called 'The Freedom to be Nothing.' The whole concept
appealed to me, because it was about letting go of a personal agenda,
and making myself totally available to Jesus, and to what He wanted
to do with me, and through me, and, therefore, indirectly, for me.
This, I believe, is what is meant by the invitation to take up my cross
every day, and to follow Jesus. His life was not about the reward
that would be his, but the benefits that would flow to each of us
who opened our hearts to the streams of graces and blessings that
flow from the Hill of Calvary.

No matter how my mind tries to side-track me, I have those constant, quieter, saner moments, when I know that I shall one day die.
I may be unsure just how best to deal with that. Should I face up to
it now, or just block it from my consciousness, and wait till it
approaches me? I would suggest that I should not wait till the end
of my life to die! I can begin the process right here, right now. I
think of Death as a pile of sand at the end of my life, which I can
take and sprinkle a little along the road of life every single day. This
involves all the many little dyings that make up the life of a
Christian. If I do this, is it possible that, when I come to the end of
the road, there's no sand left?! My dying will have been done long
ago. I often feel that the concept of the cross is frequently misunderstood. A tragedy, an illness, a death is often referred to as a great
cross. I do not accept this. Such things happen to pagans and to animals, for whom the cross has no meaning or significance. The cross
is always a source of blessing, and of redemption, and is, uniquely,
the preserve of the Christian. I would suggest that a cross is anything I do because of my decision to follow Jesus, to be led by Him,
and to carry out his commands. Because I am a Christian, I just have
to forgive you, to listen to you, to share with you, and to be there for
you. Because I am a Christian, I am not doing you (or God) any
favour, because I have no choice in this. The water of my Baptism is
placed in the chalice at Mass, one drop at a time, as I carry out my
Christian commitment to spend my life in the service of others.

Just as a terminally ill person could request 'Please send me the
flowers while I can still smell them', so, I am suggesting that I should
do the good now, while I still have the time. People like Thérèse of
Lisieux or Padre Pio said that their real work would begin after they
died. I accept and believe that, because of the way they spent their
time during their lives. When I consider the extraordinary level of
giving and of goodness that marked their lives down here, and
when I hear that their real work is to begin after they die, I am in awe
at the prospect of the goodness that will be part of the life that awaits
us all. There is nothing I will get when I die that I'm not offered now.
Heaven begins now. God doesn't send me anywhere when I die.
Rather will he eternalise the direction my life is taking right now. I
believe that, when I die, I will be amazed to see how much of my
eternal destiny was placed in my own hands!

Heavenly Father, Father of all time, I cannot hope to have any idea of what time really is. I do, however, have a genuine desire to be as alive as I can just now. I ask you, through your Spirit, to enlighten me with whatever it takes to have a profound reverence for the gift of time, and for the gift of the present moment. Please help me make full use of the graces and opportunities of the time afforded me. Thank you. Amen.

10. Not just now

Everybody wants to go to heaven, but nobody wants to die! The three stages of life are the womb life, the womb of life, and the fulness of life. There is a direct parallel between the umbilical cord being cut, and the straps being pulled up out of the grave, after the coffin has been lowered. The first can be followed by a grieving called post-natal depression, while the second is followed by bereavement. As soon as a baby is born, it can be stated that there is only one thing certain in the future of this person: she will one day die. This baby is born to die. Only then will this person arrive at being what he/she was created to be. Only when people have entered into that third and final stage of life have they become all that they were created to be.

It is often much easier to refer to all of this in the third person! 'I shall one day die' can be too close for comfort! An elderly husband and wife agreed among themselves that when one of them died, the other should mourn for a certain length of time, and then use the insurance money to have a good holiday. They were of one voice on this, and it seemed a reasonable and common-sense thing to do. After a pause, the husband remarked, 'Do you know what I was thinking? I was thinking that when one of us dies, I'm going to tour all of Europe!' Isn't it funny how it's always the other guy's death I read about in the paper! However, one day the bell will toll for me! George Burns, the American comedian, at 98 years of age, said that the first thing he did every morning was check through the death columns of the paper, and, if his name was not there, he got up!

Self-preservation is the most basic human instinct, and, therefore, the whole idea of death is not something that could possibly have any natural attraction for a human being. It just goes against the grain to face up to death. Nowhere is our faith more supportive and

more necessary than in dealing with the concept and the reality of
death. There is a line in Scripture (Heb 12:2) that gives a rule-of-life
for Christian living. 'Because of the joy that lay in the future, he
willingly went to the cross, and died for us, and he now sits at the
right hand of God.' This is a whole way of living, a whole way of
being. It is the deferred gratification that is so highly recommended
for a disciplined life. I have a goal, a target to be reached, a position
to be achieved. Only if I keep my eyes fixed on the prize will I succeed in maintaining the struggle in that direction. If I have a 'why?'
for doing something, I will always be willing to deal with the
'how?' I began this reflection with the words 'everybody wants to
go to heaven, but nobody wants to die'. However, like Jesus,
because of the joy that lies in the future, we must face up willingly
to death, as being the only way to get into the Promised Land. Jesus
is our Moses, and he has promised to lead us all the way back home
to the Father.

> A very wealthy man came with an unusual request to a priest
> who had a reputation for holiness, and for having a hot-line to
> God. The man wanted the priest to find out, in prayer, if he, the
> rich man, was going to enter heaven when he died. The request,
> indeed, was strange, but the priest, who was up to his neck in
> debt because of church building, was greatly tempted by the
> offer of a lot of money if he accepted the request. He agreed to
> take on the task.

> A week later the man returned to enquire if there was an
> answer. The priest told him that he had the answer. It involved
> good news and bad news, and he asked the man which he wanted
> to hear first. The man thought for a while, and then, with a deep
> breath, and with fingers crossed, he asked what the good news
> was. The good news was yes, he was going to heaven when he
> died. He was delighted, and absolutely thrilled. If this was the
> good news how on earth could there possibly be bad news?
> However, he looked at the priest, and asked what the bad news
> was? 'You're going to-night', replied the priest.

To be honest, on first hearing it, that is bad news! I imagine, however,
that, at a certain age, that becomes good news. I have spoken with
elderly people who have more relatives and friends who have gone

before them, than those coming along behind. I found them to have some sort of divine home-sickness, and most of their thoughts were forward, rather than backward-looking. There is an exercise that is somewhere in between contemplation and mental prayer, which, for simplicity, I call reflection. Reflection nourishes and informs the soul. It is a time of gentle revelation, and a time of disclosure. It is at such times that the reality of heaven can come to the forefront of my thinking, and can take its place in any reflection on life. After all, heaven is my home, and that is my destiny. A deep personal realisation and acceptance of this falls upon me like the dew from heaven. It comes dropping slowly and gently during those moments of quiet reflection. It is as if I can have my own personal Pentecosts, again and again. Nothing dramatic, but really profound.

When I travel to some place, it helps if I know the way! Jesus is the only way to heaven, and no one can come to the Father in any other way. Part of the afore-mentioned reflection must surely be my sinfulness, my brokenness, and my mortality. When I get in touch with this, and face up to the reality it presents, I must surely look to Jesus, who alone can bring me safely home. By myself, I don't have what it takes to get to heaven, or to live there. As a human, I am subject to the law of gravity, only capable of sinking further into the quicksand of my own selfishness. The Spirit of God is like helium gas that gives lift-off, and makes it possible for me to rise above the limits of my own nature. 'Humus' is the Latin for clay, hence the word 'human'. 'Humilitas' means 'of the ground', and humility is nothing more than the simple acceptance of things the way they are. In lifting me to a higher plain, I can see things differently. It is only natural to cling to this world, to the things I can see, touch, taste, and possess. We are sensuous creatures, taking our bearings in life through our senses. Death is about venturing into the unknown, where my passport is faith, and my visa is hope. It is only through the working of God's Spirit in me that my faith can grow to such an extent that my trust in God is total.

If God deserves anything from us, it must surely be our total trust. Jesus said that unbelief in him was the sin of this world. Whenever he encountered faith, you could always expect miracles. On the other hand, when he returned to Nazareth, he couldn't work any miracles there, because of their lack of belief. Mary is our example, above all others, of trusting God totally, and in saying a 'Yes' to whatever he asked of her. She herself didn't actually do anything. Rather she allowed God do whatever He wanted with her. For such a person, whose life was a constant series of 'Yes ... Yes ... Yes', then the final 'Yes' to death would, indeed, be easy. To breathe my last, like Jesus, commending my soul into the hands of God, with a total 'Yes' to whatever he wants for me, must be the greatest possible prayer for a human being.

As I said earlier, the road to heaven is heaven, in so far as God offers me nothing after I die that's not available to me now. The more open I am to his gifts and graces now, and the more I am in touch with my hunger and thirst for what he offers, the more of heaven enters my heart now. Just as we sometimes say that home is where the heart is, so it is possible for heaven to be where the heart is. My heart can be a prayer-room, an Upper Room, a place of the Spirit, a Pentecost place. Heaven is wherever God is, and for the one who lives life with this reality, the news that I'm going to such a permanent condition for all eternity must be the greatest possible news for any human being to hear.

> *Lord Jesus, I do believe in the moment of grace, a moment when you are passing by, and I am faced with a decision. Please, Lord, through your Spirit, help me rid myself of the tendency to put off, to delay, to neglect. I pray that your Spirit may continue to show me how I sin through neglect and omission, just as much as the wrongs of my words and actions. Thank you, Lord. Amen.*

11. Not everything I want

Human appetites can so easily become addictive and compulsive. There is an empty space inside, a sort of hole-in-the-heart, that can only be filled by God, and any attempt to fill it with something other than God will give rise to serious problems. Because the space can only be filled by God, it is like a dark hole, a bottomless abyss. Human appetites, when used in an attempt to fill this space, can grow to monstrous proportions, without doing anything to satisfy the hunger, which can be satisfied by nothing less than God. Addictions and compulsions relative to food, alcohol, drugs, sex, money, etc. are all examples of what can happen when appetites and self-will run riot.

Life is not about having everything. There can be a vast difference between what I want and what I need. I frequently find myself looking at some item in a shop, and even heading towards the check-out with it, when I realise that I don't really need it; in fact, I don't need it at all! Making this distinction is a fundamental part of the training of very young children. Pity the child who is given everything that's requested! The child is provided with basic and essential services, without having to plead or beg. There is a line, however, and it is important that the child is brought to recognise it, when the item requested is refused, and is not provided. This is a basic lesson in the facts of life. It is morally wrong to give a child unreal or enlarged expectations, because life will not always measure up to that level of satisfaction. A wise parent will ensure that the child has a first-hand experience of going-without, of doing without, of mild and occasional deprivation. Living with such experiences is just as important, and often more formative, than living with plenty.

A man died and found himself in a place that was far from

pleasant. When he was hungry, a young lad entered the room with a tray of food. Something similar happened when he was thirsty, and was provided with a large selection of drinks. When he felt tired, the young lad returned immediately, a button was pushed, and a bed emerged out of the wall, and he was invited to avail of the bed for a rest.

After some days of this, the man began to notice something different. He found out that, even if he only slightly desired something, while not really wanting it, and certainly not needing it, it was provided immediately. This puzzled him, and, in some strange way, annoyed him. It all seemed so unreal, and so programmed, that it smacked more of robotic exercises than of something with a spirit, or a heart. He called the young lad and asked him 'Tell me this: Can I do without something here?' 'Oh, no, that's not allowed,' came the reply. 'But, I mean something I just thought of for a second, but I don't want it or need it, do I have to have it?' 'Oh, yes, that's the rule here.' 'And is this going to go on for all eternity?' asked the man, with a sense of exasperation. 'Yes, it will continue day in, day out, for all eternity.' 'Oh, no,' replied the man. 'If that's the case, I'd be better off in hell.' To which the young lad replied 'And where do you think you are?'!!

I am grateful to God for many things in life, not least the family in which I grew up. I was/am one of a family of thirteen children. Our home of origin was a simple, safe, and secure nesting-place, where the currency was love, and the bank manager was God. I learned from an early age that richness has little to do with money. In my innocence, I thought we were poor, and it has taken the intervening years to let me see just how rich we were. I distinctly remember feeling sorry for a cousin of mine, whom we considered rich, because he got a gold watch for his tenth birthday. A gold watch at ten would leave few surprises for his twenty-first!

Jesus speaks very clearly about how wealth and riches can come between us and God, and make our journey to him all the more difficult. Materialism can choke the spiritual life. I remember, when first learning the Ten Commandments, considering idolatry and false gods so remote as to be unreal. That particular Commandment had some relevance in the time of Moses, but certainly not in Ireland today! The intervening years have changed my opinion on that, I can assure you. I've seen many an instance when the god was very false indeed, while the worship was real, and the commitment was total. For example, if we look at a country like Poland, which is now recovering from years of oppression and hardship, and is gradually becoming wealthy and prosperous. It should not be surprising, therefore, that the traditional Polish allegiance to God and to church should begin to wane in exact proportion to the growth in materialism. That's what I mean by materialism choking the spiritual. It is difficult to serve God and mammon. Jesus said that the poor in spirit were blessed. It would be a grave mistake to canonise poverty in itself, which is certainly not always a good thing. Jesus is speaking about detachment, where I possess the wealth, rather than the wealth possessing me. It is a question of which kingdom I'm living in. In the kingdom of God, Jesus is Lord, and money is often lord in the kingdom of this world.

Spirituality is based on the simple fact that only God can do God-things. God provides the fulness, if I provide the emptiness. It is a strange paradox that the more I empty myself of self, the more God's Spirit fills the space vacated, until, like Mary, I could become full of grace, or full of God's life. Herein in true and eternal riches and wealth. This, indeed, is the pearl of great price, which, when I find it, I should willingly give up everything else to possess it. This is treasure in heaven, where the rust cannot destroy, or the moth consume. To see this as being the only wealth worth pursuing is directly the result of the work of God's Spirit in my heart. The Spirit of Truth, in bringing me into all truth, reveals this great and vital news to me. Flesh and blood could never do that, because flesh and blood can understand only flesh and blood.

I am hoping that you, the reader, when you reflect on the story in this chapter, will see just how this could be hell, when every whim and fancy is satisfied, and there is no desire that cannot be indulged. For me, the real hell would be that everything would be coming in my direction, without anything going out to others. It is significant to note that the 'others' do not exist in the story, beyond the young lad who functions like a slave. How true it is that it is better to give than to receive. I always think that the happiest people on earth are those who do not have a great deal themselves, but who constantly share the richness of themselves with those around them. They are continually being drawn out of themselves, towards others, rather than making themselves the centre of their world, expecting everyone else to rotate around them. They are out-going people, in every sense of that word. Total selfishness is a very real form of solitary confinement, where the only person in my world is myself. Selfishness is the worst form of loneliness, in that it is self-inflicted, and self-inflating. There is no room in my life for anyone else, including God. Everything and everyone is there to meet my needs, and when they have served that purpose, they can be discarded. My idol, my false god, is now much nearer home, because I myself have become that idol. That's frightening in its ramifications. I even expect God to conform to my expectations. God becomes God in my life the very instant I cease playing God.

Lord Jesus, I believe that you know me through and through. That's what helps me cope when I become aware of things in me that I don't like. I don't like my need to collect, to hoard, to cling to things. If I am to change, then I just have to turn this over to you. Lord, for anything like this in me that is not from you, I declare my total willingness to let go. I depend on you, please, to avail of that good-will. Thanks, Lord. Amen.

12. Preparing the way ahead

Over the years when sisters, relatives, and friends of mine were having their families, I often found myself in a dilemma. I so much wanted to get something, in preparation for the new baby, but I was always a little nervous that all might not go well, and I was more inclined to wait till after the birth, and then present the gift. I admired the ability of people to even have a special room ready for the new arrival, as well as cot, pram, nappies, and feeding utensils. There was a lot of preparation put into the time of waiting, and all this was accepted as part of the process. At the other end of life, I have come across individuals who had every detail worked out for their funerals well in advance of that time. A preference is expressed about readings at Mass, who does what, and other details of the funeral. Once again, I admire those who can be so practical and down-to-earth about something that is more than literally down-to-earth.

There is a much more vital and important preparation for death, of course, that is part of the very life of every Christian. This has to do with plugging fully into the reservoir of God's grace that is ours because of Calvary. It has to do with fully accepting Jesus as my personal Saviour, in the sure and certain belief that he, and he alone, will bring me safely home. I like the story about the thief on the cross on Calvary, who asked for help, and was offered heaven. We speak of pure gift here, where God is the giver, and we are the receivers.

I often think that Jesus is more interested in our decisions than our discussions. He won't send me anywhere when I die. Rather will he eternalise the decisions I now make. If I decide to live with him now, then I will live with him for eternity. My future is in the present. While speaking, of course, of spiritual wealth, I am laying up stores now where the moth cannot consume, nor the rust destroy. This is not about achievement, it is about goodwill, and about letting go. The first thing I have to do is to stop playing God. Immediately I do that, God takes over, and I'm on my way to the fulness of life. A very wealthy man died, and went to heaven. He was surprised and not a little annoyed to find that he was given a mere hovel in which to live, while another man, whom he knew to be a humble labourer, was given a mansion. When he enquired the reason for the apparent discrimination, he was told that the living quarters are provided by whatever material each person had sent on ahead during life! That story limps if taken literally, of course, because it is never a question of contributing to my own reward. My main contribution to that reward is keeping the door of my heart open, and confirming my daily availability to Jesus and to his plan and purpose for me. This ensures that I meet the conditions that lead to the reward. The preparation for the third stage of life is more a question of attitude than act. It is not earthly currency, either in money, achievement, human endeavour, or personal success. It is being open to accept and receive gift.

The king was a king, and a proper king indeed. The fool was a fool, and an equally proper fool. One day the king handed the fool a stick, with the words 'Take this stick, and mind it with great care. If, however, you meet someone who is a greater fool than yourself, give the stick to that person.'

The years passed. The king grew old, and was on his death-bed. He summoned his family, his courtesans, his army chiefs, and his faithful fool. He told them he was about to embark on a long journey, from which he would not return. He would be setting out on that journey shortly, and he wanted to take leave of them. There was great consternation and weeping. In the midst of it all, the fool approached the king, and asked 'Majesty, on all other occasions when you set out on a journey, either within this country, or to another country, you always made detailed preparations for the journey. You sent couriers and soldiers ahead to prepare the way for your coming, and to ensure that everything was in readiness. Pray, then, tell me, what preparations have you made for this, the longest and most important journey of your whole life.' 'Alas', said the king, 'I have made no preparation for this journey. I kept putting off doing anything, and now it is too late. I just don't have time.' 'In that case, Majesty, take this stick, because, at last, I have found a fool much greater than myself!'

I was born to die. All of my earthly journey is moving inexorably towards that final destination. I remember, as a child, we had a prayer against 'a sudden and unprovided death'. I also remember reading a death notice in the paper of a man aged 97, and what caught my eye was that the notice said 'unexpectedly'! The more I reflect on the truth of death, the more obvious it is to me that God has more than gone out of his way to help me meet that destination with single-mindedness. O.K., there is a form of perverse blindness in our natures than prevents us seeing or hearing what we don't wish to see or hear. There is a tendency towards insanity, that enables us continue doing the same thing, and to keep expecting some different result! I see God's Spirit as being central here. Because of original sin, there is some sort of basic rebelliousness within us, and, while I might not publicly admit to it, there can be some sort of futile hope that I am destined to be the one exception in the final shake-down of the human race! In a way it would be funny, if it were not so stupid. Sometimes I imagine God smiling rather than crying when he looks at us, because we're often more stupid than evil!

When I worked in a parish, and, therefore, would frequently have Baptisms, I used catch the water in a little bowl, as it was being poured, and later put it in a small bottle, which the parents would take home with them. To the Hebrews, water was more a sign of death than life, and it is very significant that they came through the waters of the Red Sea to get into the Promised Land. Jesus would later walk on water to show his authority over death. Through the use of water in Baptism, the child is set on the journey of dying. As a Christian, every time I put someone else in front of myself, I die a little to my own pride and my own selfishness. There is no greater love than this form of dying for the sake of others. Just as life is something that is made up of all the days along the way, so death is something that can be part of every day. In my struggles to love others, to keep my own selfishness from getting in the way, to be a person to whom others are important, I continue to die to myself every single day of my life. If I do that, I'm not waiting for the end of the journey to die, because my dying will have begun long ago, and most of it might well be done by then. On the other hand, if I wait till the end of my life to die, it could well be too late. 'Father, if it's possible, let this chalice pass from me ...' The chalice represents the death of Jesus. Into the wine I place a drop of water, to represent the water of Baptism, to show my willingness to join all my little dyings to the death of Jesus. Otherwise, those dyings have no value. Joined to the death of Jesus, they take on an eternal value, and become part of the process of redemption. In this way I can really share in the offering of Calvary, where I join my 'yes' to Jesus to his 'yes' to the Father. This is certainly a daily and realistic preparation for the final journey up ahead.

Lord Jesus, there are times when it all looks so simple! Then, for some reason, I lose the vision, and get all tied up in problems! Please, Lord, help me fully accept the simple truth that living with you and for you is my surest way of being with you always. I ask that your Spirit continually remind me that it all begins here and now. Please don't let me ever be separated from you. Thank you, Lord. Amen.

13. You'll find what you are

It is a true statement that, in life, the miles stretch ahead of me, but the things that trip me up are inside me. I sometimes imagine some sort of slide-projector in the brain that projects all my inner personal images onto others, and other situations, and makes it appear to be someone else's problem. It can be very difficult, and sometimes impossible to be objectively honest. Just as I may have to stand back from an oil painting to see it properly, so can I be too close to something to see it as it is. This inability to see, often accompanied by an unwillingness to see, is evidenced at its most sinister in bigotry, racism, and all forms of intolerance. There are none so blind as those who don't want to see.

After St Paul's encounter with Jesus on the road to Damascus, Ananias laid hands on him, by way of a blessing, and 'immediately something like scales fell from his eyes, and he could see.' This is truly significant, and is a highly symbolic way of describing being healed of spiritual blindness. The story of the journey to Emmaus on Easter morning is another powerful example of blindness being healed. The disciples travelled with Jesus, listened to him, and talked with him, but they did not recognise him. Suddenly, after he broke bread with them, 'their eyes were opened', and they knew it was Jesus. Nothing had changed, except their ability to see. Spiritual blindness is a very real form of blindness, and is a condition that requires nothing short of a miracle. 'Lord, that I may see', the prayer of Bartimaeus, is a prayer that could come from the heart of any one of us. A genuine desire to see is all that is required. The Lord works powerfully when there is good-will present. He fills the hungry with good things, and when there is a genuine hunger in the heart, the Lord is more than willing to act on that. I often imagine that when I pray 'Lord, that I may see', God judges the depth of that prayer, by looking beyond the words, to discover just how genuine and how real is my actual desire to see.

'Prejudice' comes from the words 'pre-judging', which involves making judgements without having the facts. This is an area of land-mines, because what is going on within me is projected onto those things around me, and outside me, and gives them a colour and a reality they do not actually possess. It is an area of land-mines, because it has the potential for great destruction and harm. Nothing short of a miracle can cure prejudice. The psychiatrist had a serious problem with one of his patients, who was convinced that he was dead. The psychiatrist tried everything to no avail. Finally, he got the patient to accept the simple fact that corpses don't bleed. When this fact had been established, the psychiatrist took a pin, pricked a tiny hole in the patient's finger, and squeezed out some blood. The patient looked at his finger for a moment, and then with total conviction, he turned to the psychiatrist with the words 'Well, what do you know? So corpses do bleed after all!'

> A man pulled up at a filling-station one day, and while being served, he casually asked the pump attendant what the people were like in the village further down the road. In reply, he in turn was asked what the people were like in that last village he had just come through. 'Oh, they were very pleasant, and most friendly', was the reply. 'In that case', replied the young lad, 'you will find the people in this next village exactly like that'.

> Shortly afterwards another man stopped for petrol, and, by a strange coincidence, asked the same question about the people in the next village. Once again, he, too, was asked about the people he had met in the village he had just come through. When he said that he had found the people in that last village to be sour, dour, and unfriendly, he was assured that he would find the people in the next village to be that way also!

This is a very good example of how some people actually do see things. If I point a finger at another, I may fail to notice that there are three fingers pointing at myself! I actually witnessed the following scene: A young lad of about seven had hit his younger sister, and she was crying. The mother, who, as it happened, was quite a big woman, lifted the young lad with one hand off the ground, gave him a smack across the side of the head with the other, and told him, 'I'll teach you not to hit someone smaller than yourself!' At the time, I felt sure the woman did not hear too well what she herself said, even though, it's possible the young lad heard the message being delivered.

Jesus is an oculist with a difference. He doesn't offer new glasses, he offers new vision. The treatment must begin in the heart, where the blindness begins. His Spirit is a Spirit of Truth, and he leads me into all truth, and only then will I be free. Bigotry and prejudice is self-perpetuating, and cannot be effectively covered over, or half-healed. It requires fundamental surgery of a kind that only God can do. Only the Creator can recreate, and what is needed here is a complete replacement of what is wrong by what is right. Most times we can see this problem much clearer by observing it in another. Take an alcoholic, for example. Everybody knows that he's an alcoholic, but he himself refuses to admit to it. The problem is that, part of the disease known as alcoholism is that it seeks to deny its own existence. This is central to the whole problem of alcoholism. If the alcoholic could see the situation as others see it, and if he accepted the facts as they are, he would have taken the first giant step towards recovery. It is an accepted and well-known fact that nothing can be done for an alcoholic until he is able to see things as they are. The facts are friendly, in that they don't change. He is an alcoholic, and, even if he never drinks again for the rest of his life, he will always be an alcoholic. It is called alcohol*ism*, not alcohol*wasm*!

It must be wonderful to be free from all delusions! The Greek word for conversion is *kinosis*, and it literally means to empty out. I think of the human soul as a deep deep well, with a bubbling vibrant spring at its base. The problem is that the well has got cluttered up with junk, garbage, prejudices, resentments, etc., etc., and the water cannot get to the surface. Conversion is a process of emptying out, in that it means getting rid of the junk bit by bit, piece by piece, so that the water can rise to the surface, and be life-giving. In practice, this is an impossible task for any human being to undertake, and nobody is more aware of that than Jesus. That is why he speaks of his Spirit being a fountain of living water that rises up from within a person, bringing to the surface all the wreckage of the past, that must be disposed of. The Holy Spirit runs the world's best rubbish-skip service, and it is totally free! This emptying process is essentially the work of God's Spirit. I always think of the Spirit being more than willing to effect this great inner change in me as soon as I give the word. I remember a man, who was quite drunk, coming to me one time, asking me to pray for him. I asked him if there was anything in particular I should pray for, and he said 'Will-power, Father, will-power'! I told him to go off home, think about it, and the following day when he was sober, and he felt he had the will, he should return to me, and, together, we would ask for the power! If I have the will, God will give me the power to do anything. It can help to imagine God's Spirit being on stand-by, ready and willing to move in with the JCB's, the earth-movers, and the skips, as soon as I give the signal. God can do nothing in me without my permission. The door of my heart has only one handle, and that is on the inside.

> *Holy Spirit, Spirit and Breath of God, I depend on you totally. You are a Spirit of truth, and I have no reason to believe that I always see the truth or act on the truth. Please heal my blindness. I offer you my honest desire to be open to the truth, no matter what it is, and I trust you to make use of my good-will. Thank you. Amen.*

14. Putting the world together

One attempt to help understand church these days is to move away from the idea of institution and buildings, and concentrate on people. A group of people gathered together out in the middle of a field can be church. When this is accepted as true, and acted on, and not just another idea, I find it can be very life-giving. I can go off for the day with a group of parishioners, and in the midst of all the fun and the play, we are being a church in action. The body Jesus had when he walked on this earth went with him when he returned to the Father. He now has no other hands, feet, or voice but ours. Our vocation is the same as Mary's, who was asked if she was willing to provide the body for Jesus, so that he could enter into our human condition, and effect redemption in us. We provide the body, and God provides the Spirit. It is the greatest possible calling for a human being. We, the people, we are the church. I remember getting a group to spell 'church' out loud, and with emphasis on certain letters: chURch. I defined church one time as something like an F.A. soccer Cup Final in Wembley, where one hundred thousand people, badly in need of a little exercise, are sitting down, very comfortably, while they criticise twenty-two poor guys badly in need of a rest! The call of today is to get down off the stands!

'No man/woman is an island', is much more than just a throw-away line. It is a fact, and, unless it is seen as that, I will never see my proper place within the scheme of things. I have a responsibility to others for my behaviour, and how I live my life. When I strive to be genuine and authentic I mediate life to others, while I am mediating death if I am deceitful and phoney. The greatest wealth in my life are the people who surround me, and it is important to value them for what they are. Another person is a gift that I can never fully know. Gifts often come in wrapping, and, of course, I wouldn't throw a gift in the bin just because I didn't like the paper in which it was wrapped. I do that when I judge people by the colour of their skin, where they live, or how they look. How often I have heard the phrase 'She's really very nice when you get to know her.'

The world in which we live is often seen as being very materialistic, and people are referred to by their functions, what they work at, what their profession is. This can prevent us seeing people as people, real living human beings. The greatest resource of any nation is people, and it is a grave mistake not to be aware of the importance of each individual. In any of our large hospitals, we are all aware of the many sophisticated and hugely expensive machines in places of intensive care. There is always a tag hanging from each machine, and that tag tells me when the machine was last checked, to ensure that it is in perfect working order. I often think it is a pity that more sensitive support is not available to the nurses, to ensure that they're O.K. After all, it is the nurses who run the hospital. The doctors are not always with a patient, nor are the machines always in use! The nurses, however, are there twenty-four hours a day, 365 days of the year.

It was a very wet Saturday afternoon. The mother had gone into town, and the dad was looking after several small children. They were restless, and he was getting frustrated. In desperation, and hoping to keep them occupied, he began to give each an assignment. In his Monday to Friday job, he was a hardnose businessman, and now he was going to try some of his time and motion experiments! For a seven-year-old, he took down a magazine from a shelf, found a map of the world in it, cut it up into many pieces, shook up the pieces, and presented Junior with a jigsaw puzzle! That would surely keep him occupied for the rest of the afternoon.

Some minutes later, while still giving assignments, he was both amazed and slightly disgusted to notice that Junior had completed the jigsaw. He asked him how he had completed the task in such record time, and he was truly amazed at the answer: 'I didn't know how to do it. All I could see were lines, colours, and all sorts of things, and I didn't know where to begin. I had never seen a map of the world before. And then, guess what, dad, do you know what happened? I just turned over one of the pieces, and didn't I discover that there was a picture of a man on the other side. I turned over all the pieces, put the man together, and that way the world came together as well'!

Over the past few years there have been frantic efforts at international level to bring peace to certain war-torn areas throughout the world. The most such efforts can ever achieve is bring an end to war. Peace, however, is certainly not the absence of war. Peace must begin in the human heart, before it can ever become a reality on the world stage. Lord, let there be peace on earth, and let it begin with me. It is my single greatest contribution to the good of people that I should make myself available to the Lord, so that he can effect in me what he came to do for the world. At Pentecost, the apostles were given the Spirit so they could go out and give witness to that fact. With the privilege comes the responsibility. The whole world is different because of the presence of each decent upright person who is open to God, and to others. How often we hear it said that all that is needed for evil people to succeed is that good people do nothing. If I'm not part of the solution, then be sure that I am part of the problem.

There is something obscene about the fact that half the world is dying of hunger while the other half is on a diet, trying to get down the weight. There is more than enough food in the world. That is not the problem. The problem is that people cannot accept the fact that we are all on this earth with equal right, and we all have an equal right to share in the earth's resources. A world order that respected the rights of people of all nations, colours, and cultures is something that only God would promote, and something that only God could make possible. We may say that all people are born equal, but we know only too well that some people are more equal than others!

One of the many striking things about Jesus in the gospel stories is his personal contact with people, and the respect and time he had for the individual. He touched the untouchables, and he spoke to those who were not to be spoken to. He broke every taboo in the book, because when it came to a choice between a law and a person, the person always took priority. There was no one, no matter how marginalised, who was outside the pale of his acceptance and respect. Don't forget, Jesus came to save the world, and he began this by reaching out to save individuals. He obviously believed that if he could save the individuals, the world would be alright.

Heavenly Father, you are Father of each and every one of us. Each is a unique individual in your eyes. What I do, or don't do, matters to you. I ask for your Spirit that I might be able to take responsibility for my place in the scheme of things. I want to be and to do whatever you had in mind when you created me. Please accept my good-will, and see your plan for me to its completion. Thank you, Father. Amen.

15. The choice is yours

In general it is right to say that life can be what I want it to be. There are, of course, twists and turns to life that are outside my control, but, in general, life is strongly influenced by my input in the mix. As with a computer, put in junk, and you'll get out junk. Life can be a series of repayments on my personal investments. It is important to take responsibility for my own life, and to be in control of my life. When I give others power over me, I am in trouble. I can spend my life making excuses, and blaming others, and holding them responsible for how things are with me. On the other hand, I can get behind the steering-wheel of my own car, and take my own decisions, and make my own choices. It is important to remember that I do have choices, and I should always be willing and ready to exercise that right. I have free-will, and I must not abdicate my right to act within the freedom of that free-will. Moral cowardice is very destructive of healthy living. On the other hand, moral courage, the rarest form of courage, is a most precious commodity in worthwhile living.

Intellectual prowess is not necessarily the same as being smart! A person could be highly intelligent, and act extremely stupid. Quite often, the intelligence becomes a hindrance, especially if it is mixed with intellectual pride, and is totally unfree. It is a freeing thing to admit that I don't know something, that I was wrong, that I acted stupidly. There would never be a war if somebody somewhere would only say 'I'm sorry, I was wrong. It was my fault.' I always have a choice in these things, but sometimes pride will not allow me make the correct choice. The more I reflect on life and living, the more I am convinced just how vital honesty and truth are, and how destructive and imprisoning are lies and deceit. Yes, indeed, 'the truth shall set you free.'

In a particular village, there was a wise old man who was looked upon as a sage. People came to him for advice and words of wisdom, and he was looked up to. There was a young lad in the village who had an opportunity of going away for an education. He came back, considered to be very intelligent, and with great book-learning. He was jealous of the old man with his wisdom. So he decided to show him up, and test him.

He decided he would get a small bird, for use in an experiment. He would hold the bird in his hand, with some feathers sticking out at one end, and the beak at the other. He would approach the old man, and begin by asking him 'Is this a bird?' Then he would ask him 'Is the bird alive or dead' If the old man said the bird was dead, he would open his hand and let the bird fly away. If the man said the bird was alive he would crush the bird in his hand, and then hand the dead bird to the old man. Either way, he was going to prove the old man wrong.

He came to the old man and said 'Now, I have a question for you. Is this a bird? What do you think?' The old man replied 'Yes, it seems to be a bird.' Now the next question: 'Is the bird alive or dead?' The old man put his hand on the young man's shoulder, and said 'That, my friend, depends totally on you.'

It is a long journey from the head to the heart. People who live in their heads are very hard to communicate with. Their criterion tends to be theories and academic knowledge rather than experience. In a way they have no heart, and can lack compassion, tenderness, and a sympathetic spirit. They know the price of everything and the value of nothing. The journey from the head to the heart is a process of formation, where the sharp edges are removed, the ego is deflated, and a mature, and more mellow approach to life, and to living, is developed. I often joke that if I knew now all I thought I knew when I was in my teens, I'd be very clever indeed! What matters in life is not contained in school texts. Experience is a very good school, but sometimes the fees are quite high. It is difficult, if not impossible, to speak seriously about life to someone under thirty-five years of age. The age chosen is arbitrary, of course, but it is suggested to make a point. Life has a way of putting me in my place, and is a constant school of learning. My own father had a way of reminding us of this, when he reminded us that he had been on this earth a little longer than us! There is an Irish phrase which says that sense doesn't come before age.

When John was five, he thought his father knew everything. When he was thirteen, he just wasn't too sure about that. When he was seventeen, he decided his father knew nothing. When he was thirty-five, he was amazed at how much his father had learned in the meantime! Probably when he was fifty, he was sorry his father wasn't around anymore to advise him! Life is a journey. When I was teaching school, I often spoke of that journey being from Tralee to Dublin. Age-wise, I was around the Curragh, while the pupils were still around Castleisland, and had not yet left the borders of Kerry! It would be unrealistic of me to expect them to admire, or even to imagine the scenery of my part of the journey! I could share my vision with them, of course, and let them know what I had dis-covered in life, while allowing them the freedom not to see any-thing of my vision.

Wisdom is not just about knowing what is right and good, but being able to apply it, and live up to it. A person could know what is correct, but might not be too wise. Sacred Scripture has a lot to say about Wisdom. The Book of Proverbs has some beautiful state-ments about wisdom. In 2:6 we read that 'Only the Lord gives wis-dom'. And then in chapter three, we read 'Happy the person who finds wisdom and gains insight. She is of more value than silver, and more precious than gold. She is more precious than pearls; nothing you could wish for can compare with her. With her right hand she offers you length of days, with her left riches and glory. She leads you through restful ways; all her roads are peace. She is the tree of life for those who clasp her; those who possess her are happy.' The remainder of this chapter contains further comments on the riches of wisdom, but what I have quoted should give sufficient indication as to where true wisdom has its source. In this area it is a question of no words being necessary for those who understand, and no words being possible for those who do not understand.

It is in the light of true wisdom that I want to show up the contrast between the old man and the young man in our story. Each side needs patience and respect for the other. The young man can help the older by holding up a mirror to reflect what the old man himself might have been like in his youth. On the other hand, the old man might help to give direction to the youth's quest for wisdom and knowledge. Maturity is not always the exclusive preserve of age. I have come across some pupils in school who, in some ways, were more mature than their parents. In general, one could say that the baby takes all that is given, and reaches maturity when he is willing to give all he can give. There is no one more loved in a family than a new-born baby. The baby just has to be, to be loved. As the baby grows older we begin to demand more of a return for our love, which is all very well, up to a point. While not making excuses for the arrogance of the youth in the story, I would suggest that our love be expressed with patience, compassion, and understanding. Life has a way of melting and moulding such arrogance, and I am grateful that I was given sufficient space at such times to make many mistakes, and to learn from them. I will summarise my honest feelings by stating that if I had a choice of being any age, I would choose to be the age I am! I must not deny the youth a similar choice, even if I feel threatened by the fact that he'd probably choose to be the age he is!

> *Spirit and Breath of God, if you weren't there to guide my steps, I would have good reason to despair! So much depends on the decisions and choices I make, and I am only too well aware of the danger of me being in control of this! I have to trust you totally, because I have no reason to trust myself. Please, please don't let me get in your way, and mess up everything. Thank you, Lord. Amen.*

16. What is happening within

There is a vast difference between religion and spirituality. Religion has to do with external practice, something we do, bound up in rules and regulations, and has a lot to do with control. Spirituality, on the other hand, is what God effects within us, when we allow him, and it has to do with surrender. I would strongly contend that God is not too interested in religion! I have a physical heart, and then I have that inner core self, where I am most myself, which is generally referred to as 'the heart'. It is this part in which God is most interested. 'These people honour me with their lips, but their hearts are far from me.' Scripture speaks of an obedient heart, and wholehearted obedience. The Psalms, with few exceptions, refer to the heart again and again. St Paul reminds us that God sees into our hearts, and he knows our every thought. Perhaps the most powerful language is used when God speaks of how he desires to change us. 'I will take out your heart of stone, and give you a heart of flesh. I will put my spirit in you ...'

A heart transplant involves two basic things. Firstly, the old heart is not capable of doing what it is supposed to do, and a decision is made to remove it. This cannot be done, of course, until there is another suitable and healthy heart available to replace it. The operation involves removing the useless heart, and transplanting the new heart. Presuming normal success in such matters, life returns to the healthy state of what it had been before the heart broke down. There is a direct parallel between this and what God wishes to do within our spirits. Because of original sin, there is a hole in the ozone layer of my spirit, and I am fundamentally and irreparably damaged. Only God, who creates, can recreate. God is not into bypass surgery! He is thorough and fundamental, and the change is permanent. 'I make all things new.'

Let us reflect for a while on the circumstances and situations in which Jesus delivered his message. There were lepers, sinners, outcasts all over the place, and they, who had nothing of themselves, were more than open to anyone who offered them hope or help. Jesus had no problem with these, and he was clearly seen to be their friend. He defended them, fed them, healed them, and they were more than willing to follow. There was another group, however, who presented Jesus with an almost impossible task. They were religious people, who had surrounded themselves with thousands and thousands of rules and regulations, and who were zealous for those rules, and both strict and proud of themselves in their observance. In effect, Jesus could do nothing with them, and it was they who eventually killed him. He tried everything to get them to look within their hearts, and to open their hearts, rather than their critical and cynical ears to his message. He really laid it on the line for them about their emphasis to external practice and behaviour, without having any inner back-up. He spoke of cleaning the outside of a cup, while inside it was stained and dirty. He spoke of white marble tomb-stones, lovely on the outside, but full of rottenness within. His words fell on deaf ears. He said that the mouth speaks out of the abundance of the heart, and he spoke of good people as those who receive his word with good and obedient hearts. In an external way, I could bless myself, genuflect, and go through a whole routine of ritual, and have nothing happening within. Such must be an abomination to the Lord.

> The little girl was six years of age, but already quite a formidable young lady. She inherited a lot of her mother's stubbornness, and from an early age, there were frequent clashes of personality. One day things came to a head. The mother grabbed a stool, placed it in a corner, and told the girl to sit there, and wait till her dad came home. She refused to sit, despite all threats, and, eventually, her mother, in sheer frustration, grabbed hold of her and plonked her down in a sitting position on the stool.

> Shortly afterwards the dad arrived home. He noticed his daughter sitting on the stool, with a look on her face that could kill. 'Well, what's this all about? he enquired, trying to be cheery. 'What are you doing there in the corner?' The reply was blurted out 'Outside I'm sitting down, but inside I'm standing up'!

It's not possible to legislate for morality. I can go through all the externals, with perfect adherence to law, and inside I can be totally unreal, and insincere. Only God can change the human heart. God's Spirit comes to dwell in our hearts, so that, from there, he can change our attitudes and our actions. Some years ago there was an advertisement for a certain kind of health salts which said 'Inner cleanliness comes first.' Indeed, inner cleanliness is the only real cleanliness. Jesus is quite direct when he compares the Pharisees to those who wash and clean the outside of a cup, while the inside is deeply stained, and full of germs. When I receive Communion, I must open my heart as well as my mouth, so that Jesus can enter the temple of my heart with a whip of cords to clear out all the buyers and the sellers. 'Freely, freely, you have received. Freely, freely, give.'

I knew a man one time, who was very simple and completely inno-cent. At forty, he would ask Santa, in the city store, for pyjamas! Anyhow, he occasionally went on diets, and this was hilarious. He was totally convinced that he actually was on a diet if nobody saw him eating! His family had a lot of innocent fun with him, because his mother would accidentally (?!) leave the where-with-all for a good meal somewhere out of sight, and, of course, it was always sure to disappear! In this case, it was totally innocent, and we can rightly smile as we speak of it. It is not a smiling matter when so-called intelligent folks play the same game, with a mind to deceive, or live a lie. Quite often, a real test of a person's character is how he acts when he is alone. The word sincere has an interesting deriva-tion. A sculptor is working on a block of marble, for example. He chips away, and the figure emerges. Supposing he accidentally chipped off a tiny corner that should not have been chipped off, he is not about to scrap the whole project. He has special filling wax, which can be shaped appropriately, and mixed with marble dust. This can harden to such an extent that it is made to look like gen-uine marble. The non-expert would never spot the flawed corner of the statue. To ensure that all of the statue was genuine, with no phoney parts, a statue had to be marked *sine cera*, without wax, from which we have the English word sincere.

Sometime one sees an elderly person, crippled with infirmities, making despairing efforts to genuflect when entering a church. The habit of a life-time. While respecting this, I use this as a good example of the central message of this present reflection. I am totally convinced that the Lord is interested only in what my heart is saying and doing when I come into his presence. It is like a long row of people, all bowing and curtsying as the queen goes by. Thank God, there's no barometer for measuring how much genuine inner courtesy is accompanying the external actions. I would contend, however, that we all come across the genuine article from time to time, the authentic genuine individual who means what is said, and who says what is meant. What you see is what you get. Such people, and, thankfully, they do not form an endangered species, always contribute to building up my trust in humanity.

Lord Jesus, I want you to make your home in my heart. I ask you, please, to feel at home, and to be at home there. I want and I need that my words and actions be controlled from within. I really want to live out my life, to have my life as something that flows out of my inner self, where you reside. May your Spirit within me touch the hearts of those I meet, either through the words I say, the prayers I pray, the life I live, or the very person that I am. Amen.

17. Life in abundance

God made us in His image and likeness, and, unfortunately, we often return the compliment! There is no way I can ever possibly understand God, and this will be just as true in heaven as it is now. Everything about us, as humans, is limited. Our vision cannot see beyond the horizon, and there are horizons on every dimension of our lives. I think of myself like someone in a magician's act, standing upright in a tall cardboard box, when, suddenly, at the click of a finger, the sides of the box fall away, and I look around in total amazement. Death must be like that. In the words of the song 'I can see clearly now.'

There is a vast difference between living and merely existing. Everybody dies, but not everybody lives. Some people just skim the surface of life, without any great depth or investment, and, when they die it is necessary to have that medically certified, because there was never much life there in the first place! Whatever one thinks of death, it must hold real fear for someone who has spent many decades on this earth, and now finds the end drawing nigh, without ever having really lived. Life is something at which I get one shot only. I have this image of the elderly, that I know is idealistic, but, hopefully, potentially true: As the body becomes more stooped, and is even seen to shrink in some way, the person inside is getting bigger, more expansive, more tolerant, and more alive all the time.

It is very very significant that Jesus says 'I came that you may have life, and have it more abundantly.' Life in abundance! What a wonderful thought, what a wonderful expression! I mentioned at the beginning how we could cut God down to our image and likeness. In doing that we would completely fail to have any idea of what Jesus has in mind when he offers abundant life, his peace, and a joy that is pressed down and flowing over. All the different expressions of God's love are described as being poured out upon us. The sacraments are rivers of grace and gift flowing from Calvary.

There once was a family that had fallen on lean times, when the family business failed, and they lost almost everything. Life in that little town became a constant embarrassment for them, because up till now they were somebody in the town, but now they had to pass the closed-down business, with the shutters up. Children can be quite cruel at times, and some of the other children at school were quite hurtful, with their snide remarks, and painful reminders.

One day a kind-hearted neighbour came to the father to enquire if there was anything that he, and the other neighbours, could do to help, and, of course, to ask if he wanted their help in the first place. The father said that he would dearly love to take his wife and children, and land somewhere in the US, where nobody would know them, and where they would have a chance to start a completely new life. The neighbour agreed to consult with his friends, and see what they could do. Several months later, they presented the family with tickets for a journey by sea from Cobh to New York.

The family had never been out of the country before, and had no idea how best to prepare for such a voyage. With their own home-spun pragmatism, they bought bread, last week's bread, which was stale but cheap. They got lettuce and cheese and filled several boxes with sandwiches. Armed with this, and their few personal possessions, they went aboard, and they all moved into the one cabin, a frightened, insecure little bunch. On the first, second, third day, when they were hungry, they ate sandwiches. On the fourth, fifth, and sixth day, the sandwiches were beginning to go off, and the very thought of sandwiches was enough to add to the sea-sicknesses most of them were experiencing. With a day or two to go before arriving in New York, one young lad was so hungry and so sick that he begged his parents to let him have a penny or two, so he could go up on deck and buy a few sweets, or something that would put a taste back in his mouth. The father gave him a few pence, and off he went. An hour latter, he had not returned, and his family was really worried. The father reluctantly had to leave the safety of the cabin and venture up on deck in search of his son. When he got up on deck, he just couldn't believe his eyes. There were rows and rows of tables, with a huge crowd of people sitting around them, eating a meal. In the middle of them was his son, with a plate piled high with chicken, potatoes, and vegetables, and he was drinking a large glass of coke. He was stuffing himself with sheer delight, and didn't notice his dad coming up behind him. The father was shocked, and growled under his breath 'Why have you done such a stupid thing? You know we cannot afford this.' The young lad's eyes lit up, as he turned to his dad, and said 'But, daddy, we could have had this every day. This was included with the tickets!'

Imagine someone arriving in heaven, looking around, and expressing amazement at the beauty and joy of it all. Jesus turns to such a person, and says 'but you could have had this all the time. This was included with the tickets.' Jesus could go on to say that he had spoken of us being invited to a banquet, and the idea of sandwiches hadn't come from him! The more I think of it, the more convinced I am that the root of the problem lies within the heart of each of us. Have you ever heard the phrase, 'That one is full of herself.' A person who is full of himself/herself has no space or place left for God's gifts. Mary was totally empty, devoid of pride or personal ambition. Therefore, she could be filled with grace and gift by God. God is the one who provides the fulness, and I am the one who provides the emptiness.

Humility is an extraordinary and intriguing concept. *Humus* is the Latin for clay, and *humilitas* is the Latin for 'of the ground'. By nature, I am subject to the law of gravity, and, of myself, I do not have what it takes to lift myself above my state, or out of the quicksand of my own selfishness. Humility is nothing more than accepting things the way they are, it is the purest of truth. It must surely be an abomination in the eyes of God for someone to become full of himself. I often hope that, perhaps, God smiles more than cries when he looks at us, because we're often more stupid than evil! It is the ever-recurring paradoxical theme of Christianity that it is in giving that we receive, and it is in dying that we are born to eternal life. Jesus tells me that if I strive to save my life, I'll surely lose it. Saving does not mean the same as preserving. Saving means holding back, not giving, not sharing, keeping myself, and what I am, to myself. There is nothing being invested here, and therefore there can be no return. It is said about computers 'Feed in junk, and you get back junk.' Life gives a very generous return on investments. The talents, when invested, always repay a full dividend. On the other hand, the talent wrapped in cloth, and buried in the ground, is stagnant and sterile, and can never be life-giving. Only if I am open to receiving life, can I ever become a life-giver. Jesus, who came that we should have life, and have it in abundance, certainly requires his disciples, in continuing and completing his work on earth, to be channels of his abundant life to others.

Heavenly Father, your love has surely been poured out in great abundance. You sent Jesus to offer us life in abundance, his joy, and his peace. You invite us into full membership of your family, calling you 'Abba', daddy. Thank you, Father for such prodigal love. I ask your Spirit to continue to reveal your generous love to me. Amen.

18. My father owns the store

Under normal circumstances, most of us function with what we have, and from where we're at. In other words, our thinking and acting is no better or worse than what we ourselves are. This 'everyday-selves-us' is highly conditioned by both nature and nurture. We are products of our environments, and we inherit a lot of the tensions, the biases, and the general way of seeing things. People who have known the hungry days seem to allow that memory compel and propel them to move as far away from that as possible, and get out of the danger of ever returning there. Such people can become very wealthy, but they can also become very materialistic, and very miserly. Some people, on the other hand, remembering their own bad days, become compassionately generous towards others less fortunate. There is no hard-and-fast rule about this, beyond saying that, one way or another, they are influenced by their own point of origin.

I often think that, when we speak of God, we need almost a whole new language. Our words are so finite, so limited, and so limiting. There is no way I can ever understand God, and that will be just as true in the next life. My most magnanimous concept of prodigal generosity would fade totally in the face of the generosity of God. St Thomas Aquinas says that whatever I say about God, there is only one thing I can be sure of: I'll be wrong, because God is much much more than anything I could possibly say of him. Jesus speaks of earthly fathers, and how they treat their children. When a child asks for bread, he is unlikely to be handed a snake. Jesus goes on to say that if earthly fathers know how to take care of their children, how much more will our heavenly Father take care of us. Like the good teacher that he is, Jesus brings his listeners from the known to the unknown. Earthly fathers is something they can understand, but the heavenly Father would be away beyond their ability to comprehend. It is not for us to get to know or understand God. That is the work of God's Spirit, through a process of revelation within our hearts. As God draws us towards himself, we come, more and more, to experience the reality of God. I would strongly contend that experience comes first, and understanding will follow. When Peter confessed that he believed Jesus to be the Messiah, the Holy One of God, Jesus told him that he was, indeed, a blessed man, 'because flesh and blood has not revealed this to you, but my Father, who is in heaven.' On another occasion, Jesus said 'No one knows the Father except the Son, and those to whom the Son chooses to reveal him.'

I come to experience God through his works, through the many expressions of his love. God could have loved me from a distance, but he chose not to. He chose to come to where I'm at, to meet me as I am. Love, by definition, is to accept the other exactly as that person is, and where that person is at. In other words, I come to experience God when I am willing to allow him come to me. This may sound simple, but it is not always so. Peter speaks for many of us, at the Last Supper, when he recoiled with horror at the thought of Jesus kneeling in front of him, washing his feet. Jesus was willing and desirous to accept Peter totally and unconditionally exactly as he was, right down at ground-level, as it were. When Peter objected, Jesus told him if he did not allow for this level of love and acceptance, he just could not be one of Jesus' disciples. Only when I allow myself experience the vastness of his love, can I possibly share with others anything of what God is. I have to 'Come and See' myself, before I can 'Go and Tell.'

It was a television show in the mid-west of the US Something similar to 'It's a Knockout' in this part of the world. Crazy competitions, where anything goes. One of the tests had three people in a supermarket, each with an empty trolley. At the sound of a whistle, they had two minutes to dash around the aisles, filling the trolleys with all sorts of goods. When the whistle sounded again, they had to go to the check-out, where all goods in each trolley were checked on the cash register. The one with the most valuable trolley was declared the winner! As they were waiting for the check-out to be completed, it was common to see someone look in another's trolley, and remark, 'Oh, I'm sorry I didn't see that. I should have taken more of those other items when I was at it.' Seldom is anyone happy with the result, because they were under such pressure that there was no time to think in the midst of the crazy scramble.

Now let us put two more trolleys into the competition, except, this time, these two, a man and a woman, are people who take Jesus seriously, and who rely and live on his promises. The whistle blows, and they're off. The usual mad scramble. One big difference this time. Our two friends are very calm as they stroll along, picking up a loaf of bread here, a pound of butter there. When one of the 'crazy bunch' drops something from a trolley, one of our friends picks it up and replaces it on the trolley. The time is up, and all six report to the check-out. Imagine the looks of the four when they peep into the trolleys of our friends! This is just too much for one of the four, who begins to berate them. 'Who on earth let you two out? Didn't anybody tell you what this is all about? Where are you going with a loaf of bread, a pound of butter, and a carton of milk? Were you not told this is a competition, and the one with the most is the winner? Where are you coming from, and what's all this about anyhow?' To which one of our friends calmly replied, 'Actually, this is all we need for today. You see, our Father owns the supermarket'!

There is a very significant element in the story of the Hebrews being led through the desert by Moses. Manna, or bread from heaven, fell every day. They gathered it each morning, and that nourished them for that day. They were forbidden to collect any for the following day, because, to do so would imply a lack of trust in God to provide for them, one day at a time. In fact, whenever some of them collected manna to store for the next day, it had gone bad, and was inedible. In the Our Father, the only prayer Jesus taught us, he tells us to pray 'give us this day our daily bread.' God is totally a God of now. 'I am who am.' In a way, I believe that this present moment is the only real time. What has gone is gone forever, and I cannot presume on a future that is not mine to control. Our two friends in the supermarket needed some bread, butter, and milk for today, and that was enough. It is said that, for the alcoholic, there is never enough alcohol. Even while pouring the present drink into him, he is planning how and where to get the next.

Each morning, when I waken up, and get out of bed, the first thing I should do is go on my knees. I thank God for the gift of today, a unique and precious gift, never before given to a human being in the history of the world. Unlike many of the boxes in which children's toys arrive, the box in which I receive the gift of today has these words written on it bold and clear: 'Batteries included.' With the day come the graces, the daily bread, needed to live that day. 'Lord, please help me believe that nothing will happen today that you and I, together, will not be able to handle.' Teresa of Avila said 'Teresa on her own can do nothing. Teresa and two ducks can do nothing. Teresa, two ducks, and God can do anything.'! God's is the power, and ours is the potential. The only limit to what God can and will do in my life are the limits I set. And it is so easy and so natural for us to set those limits, because we ourselves are so limited in every way. Sometimes we come across another human being who has a heart as big as all the great outdoors. Such a person is awesome, because this is not the norm. If I could imagine all the generosity in the world, all the generous instincts in the hearts of all God's people, I would have taken a giant step towards, while still being several giant steps short of, understanding the prodigal generosity of God. I learned to walk by walking, and to talk by talking. I will learn to trust God's care for me by practising that, one day at a time. At the beginning of each new day, I can accept the gift that it is, with the batteries or daily bread that comes with the day. I then get on with it, expecting that it will fulfil its promise. At night, I can return the day to God, and trust him to take care of any brokenness that was part of how I lived it. That day has been like a miniature life, from the birth of the morning to the sleep of the evening. Tomorrow is another day, and it will be provided with its own bread for the journey. In the words of an ad for bread 'Today's bread today'! After all, I don't need to hoard for the future, because my Father owns the supermarket, and I can return there each day.

Heavenly Father, you certainly own the supermarket! Having given us Christ Jesus, I know that you will surely give us everything else. I depend on your Spirit to lead me into a deeper awareness and consciousness of your daily love and care. I need constant reminding, because, left to myself, I tend to drift back into my worrying ways. I thank you, Father, and I really do want to know your love. Amen.

19. Hope, belief, or faith

It is said that there's a little atheist in all of us! We might not want to admit to it, but, there are times when we wonder if it's all a joke, and if we're not living in a fools' world. Like the motor-cyclist riding the wall of fire, we have to keep going full-steam ahead, lest we slow down enough to risk falling into oblivion. The atheist wants the proof, and that may then be followed by belief. The person of faith, on the other hand, accepts the truth, in the expectation that the proof will follow. It's like Jesus saying 'Unless you see signs and wonders, you will not believe', as against if you believe you will see signs and wonders. Thomas believed because he saw, and he touched. Jesus told him 'Happy are those who have not seen, and yet believe.' The atheist in us shows itself in many ways. I remember occasions in Medjugorje when I came across people who seemed to be there in search of the abnormal, and the unusual. Our Lady told the visionaries that the signs were for unbelievers, and yet these people would strongly object if they thought they were classified as unbelievers! I remember hearing a story about Saint (King) Louis of France. He had been to Mass and was having his breakfast, and there was another Mass down in the chapel for the courtiers and other staff. Suddenly one of his household came rushing in, saying 'Come quickly, your majesty, Jesus has just appeared in full bodily form at the altar after the Consecration.' The king was unmoved, as he told the messenger that he believed Jesus was always there after every Consecration. He said he didn't need to go down for proof of that fact, and that the messenger should bring to the chapel only those who did not really believe that truth.

Nowhere is our faith and trust more tested and more basic than in the whole area of death, when we leave a world we know to pass on to something that is beyond anything we could imagine. There is a sense of free-fall about this, in that we just hope somebody catches us, or we're into a nose-dive for the rest of eternity! Is it possible that life itself is a novitiate or formation programme for just that event? I believe that I can experience a certain amount of daily free-fall in my everyday walk with God. Not, of course, if I insist on being in control! The first thing I have to do is to stop playing God. I am often invited by life to step out in faith, and hope against hope that the ice is thick enough. Of course, if I am a person who never takes risks, then I am someone who never lives. I can actually practice trusting God in the simplest little ways. Then, in the words of Jesus, my faith begins like a tiny grain of mustard seed, (which is so small that it is impossible to pick it up with your fingers), and, through daily use and exercise, it will grow to become a huge tree, in which others will find shelter. So often others depend on our faith. They ask us to pray for them. They panic, and lose hope. In the gospel, the people brought their sick to Jesus, some of whom were probably unconscious, and incapable of having faith, and 'Jesus marvelled at their faith.' As a result of this journey of faith, I have come across some people who were totally at ease to close their eyes in death, because every day of their lives up till now, and their every experience of God up till now, had prepared them for this moment.

There were twin boys in their mother's womb. After some time, they became aware of each other, and of the cord that bound them with their mother. They remarked that their mother must really love them to share her own life with them. After some more time, they became aware of little nails, and some hair appearing on their heads, and they wondered what this could mean. One of them said that they were getting ready to be born. This sent a shiver of terror down the spine of the other, who exclaimed 'I don't want to be born. I want to stay where I am.' 'But you have to be born. We cannot remain on here forever.' 'I don't want to be born', repeated the other. 'How do you know there's any life after this? Have you ever seen anyone who was born. Has anyone ever come back to tell us?' 'Well, I don't know, but there just has to be life after this. It would make no sense at all if this is the end, before we've had a proper beginning. There just has got to be a life after this.' 'How do you know there's a mother?' the other asked. 'What does she look like? Have you ever seen her? I bet we have just invented her to take care of our own insecurity.' And so, the argument went back and forth. One was already a little atheist, while the other was a person of faith, which means simply that he had proof for nothing! Anyhow, the time arrived, and they were born. Shortly after birth, when it was safe to do so, they opened their eyes, and found themselves looking into the eyes of their mother. It filled their hearts with profoundest joy, and indescribable delight. They looked across at each other, as if to say 'Weren't we really stupid! How could we possibly have imagined anything like this?'

Humility is nothing more than accepting things the way they are. When it comes to God, and to his plans, I am like a tiny fish in the middle of the Atlantic ocean, swimming around, gaining new experiences of the same sea, but totally unable to rise above the sea to get an over-all glimpse of the whole thing, from shore to shore. In fact, while such would not be possible, it would be foolhardy to try, because the poor little fish wouldn't live long outside of its own environment! We can smile as we reflect on the unborn twins, and the futility of their arguing, while we may often hear something similar, as adults attempt to intellectualise about the stage of life that is still before us. 'Nobody comes back. Have you ever seen any of them? How do you know there's a God? What does he look like?' We are called to live with faith, and await the proof. Pride is a major barrier at this stage, because the human mind may not willingly accept the simple truth that there is an infinity of fact and knowledge that is well beyond its ability to comprehend, or analyse. The wise man is the man who knows just how vast is the knowledge that he doesn't know! The tiny fish in the Atlantic ocean may be a difficult analogy to accept! It is powerfully significant that Jesus invited us to become as trusting as little children, where intellect, reason, and knowledge, take second place to the security and assurance of experience, and on-going creative love. The faith of a child is a direct response to the love received. The child won't trust everybody, and may even cry when approached by someone who has not yet merited trust. Faith is a response to love, whether it's faith in God, or others.

In various and in different ways, in these reflections, I am suggesting that I should have an openness to experiencing God, and his working in my life. I should not wait till the end of my life to die! I can deal with that every day along the way. I can be open to my own particular judgement, as I stand before God in prayer today. I can listen with my heart, and say 'Speak, Lord, your servant is listening', as I go aside to pray. God is more than willing to reveal himself to me, once he sees that I am willing to be open to him. Without wishing to be morbid, I can reflect, as I prepare to doze off at night-time, on the actual surrendering of myself into the arms of God, which are so much more secure than the arms of Morpheus! I can turn my will and my life over to God every moment of every day. In fact, if I insist on running the show myself, and keeping control over my own will and my life, I will be in serious trouble. It would be a great pity, therefore, and unpardonable folly, to hold onto everything until it is taken from me! I'm going to have to die anyhow, and it would be much better to do so willingly, and with good grace!

Heavenly Father, thank you for the great gift of life. I accept it as total gift, and I am willing to give it my best shot, because I know that you have given me your Spirit to guide my steps. I don't need to know or to understand a great deal about life. All I ask for is the grace to know that I am safe in your love, and that all will be well, and all manner of things will be well. Thank you, Father. Amen.

20. Have given you authority

The last book of the Bible is called Revelations, which, basically are visions and messages received and recorded by John the Apostle in his old age. Chapter 12 is well worth reflecting on, because it deals with something that has had a profound effect on our human condition, and on our world. It recounts the struggle in heaven between Michael the archangel and Lucifer, which resulted in Lucifer (or Satan) being thrown down to earth. Note that these words are used a few times in this chapter. It would be a great mistake to think that Satan is in hell. No, he is alive and well, and living on this planet earth. Your daily papers should give you convincing proof of this! When Jesus came, he called Satan 'the prince of this world'. On one occasion, Satan took Jesus up on a high mountain, and offered him the kingdoms of this world if he would adore him. Those kingdoms were Satan's to give. There is a story in the gospel of a man who was possessed by a whole legion of demons. When Jesus was ordering them out of the man, they begged him not to send them down into the abyss. For some reason best known to himself, Jesus allowed them enter a herd of swine, and all of the herd raced for the cliffs and threw themselves into the sea. It would appear that, at the end of time, Satan will be sent the rest of the way, as it were, when he will no longer be able to peddle his lies, or to harm any of God's people.

The story in Revelations speaks of the demon waiting on the woman to give birth to a child, so that he could destroy the child. When the child was delivered from this danger, the demon then declared war on the woman. When she, in turn, was brought beyond his reach, the demon then declared war on her children. Our theology has always thought of the woman as Mary. The contrast has always been made between Mary and Eve. When Adam and Eve fell for the lie in the Garden they came under new management. They came under the sway of Satan, the father of lies. Satan's original downfall resulted from pride and an unwillingness to obey, because of the submission that such would entail. In order to counteract that poison or infection, God created a perfect antibody or antibiotic, and this is how we can think of Mary. She was everything that Satan was not. Jesus said that we are either for him or against him. This is a straight decision facing all of us. The only advantage Satan has is one of numbers! On his side are all those deliberately involved in evil, as well as those who are just looking on, uninvolved in anything. If I am not part of the solution, then, be sure, I am part of the problem!

It was a Monday morning, and, as can happen on a Monday morning, it didn't get off to a good start. Whatever John said to Mary, he soon realised that he shouldn't have said it! He had the nose bitten off him. One look at her, and fully aware of her recent mood swings, he knew this was going to be one of those days! He filled his lunch-box, and got out of there as quickly as he could.

The children, however, were not so smart. One lad was doing his home-work in the middle of the cornflakes, one girl couldn't find her socks, and another was looking for money for school books, ... and they were already late for school! The atmosphere in the kitchen was becoming more heated by the minute! Eventually, instead of the loving parting hug, the children were 'turfed' out the door! They were quite upset, and, on the way to school, when they met some friends, they began to take it out on them. Later in class, not only did Junior not know the answer, he hadn't even heard the question, and he found himself thrown out of the class-room. By 11.00am, what had happened in their kitchen that morning was beginning to effect half the parish!

Meanwhile, back in the kitchen, the mother was still in her dressing-gown! Ten cigarettes and ten cups of tea later, and it was just becoming more impossible to get this day off the ground! And then, suddenly, it dawned on her. Not one thing that happened in this house this morning had come from God. That shocked her, because she was essentially a good person. She got down the bottle of holy water, sprinkled it generously all over the place, and ordered Satan to go to you-know-where!

(He's the only one you're allowed say this to!) Anyhow, the cloud lifted, as it always will, when we use the authority Jesus gave us. Shortly afterwards, she phoned her husband, and assured him it was quite safe to come home!

That was a close one! If she had continued to forget the authority she is given as a Christian, then, who knows, but a week or two later she could be on Librium, Valium, or alcohol. I have seen many people go down the chute into the scrapyard of life, because they either forgot, or did not know their birthright as Christians. Once Jesus came up out of the river Jordan, after his baptism, when he formally took on the whole burden of sin, and where he was anointed with the Spirit in visible form, from that moment onwards the battle with Satan was in full fury. He was led by the Spirit out into the desert, and, of course, Satan was waiting for him there. Again and again, we read of Jesus ordering Satan to leave the possessed person, something Satan just had to do, even though he usually tossed the person all around the place in stubborn anger, before doing so. Satan tried everything within his power to thwart the plans of Jesus. Some of those attempts seem strange. For example, on more than one occasion he proclaimed Jesus to be the Son of God! Strange testimony from Satan! However, Jesus would have none of it. Knowing Jesus is God is not faith! It is what I do with that knowledge that can become an expression of faith. Knowledge in the head can be nothing more than mental assent, whereas faith is in my feet! Faith is expressed by what I step out and do, because of a conviction in my heart.

Jesus says in Luke's gospel (chapter 10) 'I have given you full authority over all the power of the evil one … nothing shall harm you.' That authority does not become mine until I begin to use it. I owe nothing to Satan. Reflect on the following scenario: A man was employed by this firm, and the owner gave him a rough time day after day. He was insulted in front of the customers and other staff. He was made to feel totally inferior, and of no consequence, not just to the firm, but as a person. His wages were miserly, and the work was slavish. One day a man entered the place, and, through observation, and some awareness of the situation, he saw clearly what was happening. He approached the employee and invited him to come work for him, an offer that was eagerly accepted. In his new job the man was someone of importance. His was a management role. He was in charge of others. He had a direct input into the running of the business, and he was very well paid for the work entrusted to him. Everything was going very well for several months. Then one day, his former employer entered his new place of employment, and immediately began to berate and to brow-beat him, as of old. Now, however, things were entirely different. He owed nothing to his old boss. He now could stand up to him, and tell him where to go, which he certainly did. He had a great feeling of self-worth and personal dignity as he claimed and asserted his rights, and he had the satisfaction and joy of seeing that his former boss was totally powerless in the face of his own new-found authority. He came out of that encounter with the feeling of being a redeemed slave!

The power that we have as Christians comes from the Spirit of God living within us. St John says 'Little children, there is a power within you greater than any evil power you will meet on the road of life.' This power is certainly not our own, and it would be seriously self-defeating to just presume on this power, or to take it for granted. Satan will always hit you where you're vulnerable. If you fail, he will try to convince you that you are a failure. If you succeed, he will try to convince you that you are invincible. Satan is a bully, and, like all bullies, he turns into a coward when we stand up to him. Jesus invites us to obey and follow him, while Satan tries everything possible to bully us into submission. Jesus told us to 'watch and pray, lest we fall into temptation.' We must always be on our guard, and we trust God's Spirit to remind us of the power that is available to us. On the level of one-to-one Satan is far too clever for any of us mere mortals. However, thankfully, we are not on our own, and we should never allow ourselves to be on our own. It is up to each of us to fully accept the power and authority entrusted to us. Most of us grew up with a basic awareness of sacramentals. Seldom did our mothers let us out the door without the sprinkle of holy water! We wore medals and scapulars before we had any idea what they signified. Now that we're older, we could do well to reflect on this part of our heritage.

Lord Jesus, again and again in the gospels you show your complete power over the evil one. At your word, even Satan must obey. Lord, by myself I am a very easy target for the cunning of Satan. That is why you gave me your authority; you gave me the right to speak in your name, and with the power of the victory of your blood. Thank you, Jesus. In your name, I continue to renounce Satan, to reject him, and to bind him. Thank you, Lord, for the protection. Amen.

21. Walking with the Lord

Again and again, in these reflections, I have stressed that God is totally a God of now. When God was asked who he was he said 'I am who am.' God has no past or no future, he is totally present now. In practice, this means that God is totally present to me at all times. In simple language, I have his full attention at every moment of every day! It is difficult for us to understand the significance of the following statement: *My relationship with God is exactly whatever it is at this very moment in time.* There was a man on another cross on Calvary who obviously had not made great use of his life for the welfare and happiness of others. He was being executed, and, by all accounts, he deserved it. However, he turned to Jesus, asked for help, and was offered heaven right there. All of his life is seen in the context of the prayer of now. Jesus tells a story about a man who hired workers to work in his vineyard. The first group was taken on early in the morning, the next groups at various times during the day, and the last group just before work ended that evening. What is surprising is that each group received exactly the same wage. This puzzled and annoyed the early-birds, and, when they complained, the man told them that that was how he did things. They who were there since morning got paid for a full day's work, and, if he chose to offer exactly the same to those who began work at the last moment, surely that was his decision to make, and no one suffered any injustice. He explained to them that that was just how he did things.

The implications of this are far-reaching. On the one hand, it would imply that there is little point in storing up goodness for some future reward. All reward from God is total gift. It is never something that can be merited or earned. It is gratuitous gift, given unconditionally, out of love. Today is a gift, and maybe that's why it is called the present! That's what I mean when I say that my relationship with God is exactly what it is at this very moment in time, irrespective of what may have gone before. The only 'yes' in my life that God is interested in is the last one I uttered.

It was a Sunday, and mam and dad were out for a walk with their little son, who alternated between a push-buggy and toddling on his own. The weather was beautiful, and everyone moved at a very leisurely pace. At times the little guy could be seen with his nose pressed against a shop window, fascinated by all the lovely things on display. At another time he was sitting on the footpath, scraping out the clay from the crevices between the flag-stones, with his tiny fingers. Once again he was coaxed to move forward with his parents, after, of course, having his fingers cleaned. Very soon he was trotting ahead of them. This could prove dangerous, because there was an intersection up ahead, so he was persuaded to slow down and walk along with mammy and daddy. Eventually, he had had it! He was tired, and there was going to be no more walking for him this day. So he plopped himself down on the footpath, without any great ceremony, and that was that! In the most matter-of-fact way his parents stopped, opened out the buggy, popped him in, and continued their stroll. It was the most ordinary and natural looking incident you could imagine, and was just exactly what was needed. The on-looker would see this as the expression of love and acceptance that it was, and nothing more. It would never enter that person's mind that the parents had, for one second, considered any other option, like, for example, terminating the relationship with this little self-willed creature! What made the simple incident special was that, what happened was exactly as the onlooker would expect to happen, having witnessed how the relationship had been expressed over the past few hundred yards. There was a sense of security about everything the little guy did that only comes as a response to felt-love.

There is nothing very profound about this simple story, yet it certainly deserves some moments of reflection. God is love, and the nearest I can ever hope to come to see God in this life is whenever I see people who love each other. The love exemplified in the story is solid, sturdy, and secure. It is not fickle, conditioned, or manipulative. I accept, of course, that the genuine love of parents for a child is a very concrete example of God's love for any of his children.

God wants to travel with us on the journey of life. Not in front of us, not behind us, but alongside us. This is called accompanying, and, when present, can be one of the more beautiful dimensions of life. Mother Teresa says that the greatest hunger in the world, even more than that for food, is the need to belong. It is a priceless treasure to have a friend or friends who give us space, and yet continue to be there for us. This space is very important. The parents in the story want the little lad to keep up with them, yet he is given enough space to look in the windows, to scrape the mud from between the kerb-stones, to plonk himself down on the sidewalk, and go on strike! Their love just swoops him along, in a totally safe and open-ended way. He is nobody's slave, nobody's possession.

A great deal depends on prayer, and especially how we think of prayer. Prayer that is about listening to God, will open us to hearing much more from God. God has very definite plans for each of us, and I am convinced that he is only too willing to let us in on those plans, if we are willing to listen. If I am willing to allow him into my life as Saviour, then I don't need to lag behind in the past, scraping the mud, and trying to make everything clean. If I am willing to allow him take over as Lord in my life, then I don't need to rush on ahead, risking the dangers by venturing on my own into the unknown. Faith is walking with God. 'I'll walk with God from this day on. His helping hand I'll lean upon.' Prayer is a school, just like the little lad in the story is in a very real learning experience. What matters is caught rather than taught. How many people are so busy with the urgent that they neglect the important? Prayer can even involve wasting time with God. It can be an end in itself, when I just give God time and space, and allow for the simple fact that this is his time.

There are times when I get tired, when I hit an air-pocket, go into a nose-dive, and lose altitude. At such times it becomes even more important to retain my honesty, and to plonk myself down on the footpath, if I want to, and expect God to pick me up in his arms, and carry me for a while! What he does for me is determined totally by the limits I keep setting to his love for me. I can decide that God does not, or should not love me beyond a certain point! That is totally my idea, and it has nothing of God in it. There is some kind of insanity within us that continues to protrude between us and

God, like a transformer that adapts, that feeds out piece-meal, as we decide. This is the opposite to being a channel of his love, something through which his love freely flows. God is the source of all good, and a channel is what conveys that good to other areas. The channel itself is never a source. 'Lord, may your presence within me touch the hearts of those I meet today, either through the words I say, the prayers I pray, the life I live, or the very person that I am.'

Lord Jesus, thank you for walking the journey with me. Thank you for your patience when I lag behind in guilt, or run ahead with worry. Please, Lord, continue to form me, day by day, one day at a time. I ask that your Spirit might stir up within me a deep confidence in knowing that you are always there, always watching out for me, always walking with me. Thank you, Lord. Amen.

22. Knowing from experience

There is a saying that applies to much of what we think about God: For those who don't understand, no words are possible, and for those who do understand, no words are necessary. I wrote 'what we think about God' rather than 'what we know about God', because knowledge of God is not something that can be quantified, or made material for examinations. At the time of writing, there is serious consideration being given to having Religion as an exam subject at the end of second-level education. This is O.K., as long as it is seen as an exam on Religious Knowledge, with very little to do with God! I could have all the theories in the world about God up in my head, and not believe in him at all down in my heart. Religious knowledge has to do with facts, theories, and information. For example, I can know that Jesus is God. That is something I know, up in my head. My response to that knowledge may be no more than mental assent, in so far as I accept that fact to be true. That is not faith! Satan knows that Jesus is God, but he doesn't respond too kindly to that knowledge. How I respond to that knowledge determines whether I have faith in it or not. Faith is in my feet, in so far as it enables me to step out, make decisions, and do things, because of the knowledge I have accepted as being true.

Theology, from the Greek words *Theos* (God) and *logos* (knowledge) is about knowledge of God, but, thankfully, it can be about so much more. I would contend that anyone who prays is a theologian, is someone who is learning more about God. Unfortunately, like all sciences, theology tends to couch truths in very abstract and nebulous definitions. Kierkegaard said to Hegel one time 'Aren't we philosophers extraordinary geniuses? We can take the simplest concept, and by the time we have put words on it, you can be sure that most people won't have a clue what we're talking about! Last week I was in Copenhagen, and, when I asked another philosopher for directions to a street not very far away, he handed me a map of Europe!'

For people of my generation, going to school in our younger days involved memorising page upon page of definitions, dogmas, and proofs of one kind or another. 'Much worse than the unbeliever's questions for which there are no answers, were the catechist's answers for which there were no questions'! (Louis Everly). We could rattle off distinctions between venial and mortal sin, temporary and plenary indulgences, fasting and abstaining, etc., and each of us became mini moral theologians in the making! I sometimes think that if I were a clever-enough moral theologian, I would never commit sin, because I could argue my case, and justify it! I may joke about this, but the very idea both disturbs and disquiets me.

'Whistle Down the Wind' is a beautiful, if simple movie. There is a group of kids playing in a hay-barn, when they come across a beggarman asleep in the hay. With his wrap-around tunic and flowing locks, one of the children is convinced that this is Jesus. He has a sick kitten at home, and he dashes home to get the kitten and bring it to Jesus, so he can heal it. Eventually, he gets the beggarman to place a hand on the sick kitten, convinced that this will make the kitten well again. Anyhow, shortly afterwards the kitten dies, and this greatly disturbs the children. Children want to know the reason for things happening, and so they were puzzled why Jesus allowed the kitten to die. This question led to another, where they wanted to know why God allows anybody or anything to die. These are serious questions, and they want answers, so off they went together down to the parochial house, to ask the parish priest.

The priest was having his tea when they arrived, but the children just pushed past the housekeeper, and went straight in to where the priest was eating his meal. Immediately the question 'Father, why does God allow people to die?' In response, the priest exploded in a veritable fire-works display of definitions, God words, theological concepts, all of which were intended to supply an answer to the question the children asked. When the priest was finished, and feeling quite happy with his impressive

and spontaneous dissertation, he proceeded to pour himself
another cup of tea. This is followed by an absolutely beautiful
scene, as the children are leaving. One little lad pulls at his sister's sleeve, and whispers 'Sure, he doesn't know either, sure he
doesn't?'!

Children have the happy knack of cutting us down to size on occasions! Many years ago when I was training to be a teacher, we had
one lecturer who would frequently call on someone to 'Explain that
now, just as you would to a backward pupil.' That sentence has
stuck with me since, and has been my greatest inspiration in
preparing and presenting talks and homilies. Naturally, I wouldn't
tell my listeners that I was speaking to them as I would speak to
backward pupils! I wrote a book some years ago, which is still
around, called *It's Really Very Simple*. I dedicated the book to a little
old lady I met as I came out of a Dublin city church one night where
I had just given a talk. She caught me by the arm, and, with total
sincerity, she whispered 'God bless you Father. I'm going to pray
for you, because even I understood what you were talking about'!

I like to think that one of the attributes of God is that he is infinitely
simple. I think of revelation as God allowing me 'to understand the
mysteries of the kingdom', as Jesus told his apostles, while the rest
hear the message in parables. 'Flesh and blood has not revealed this
to you, but my Father who is in heaven' Jesus told Peter, after Peter
had confessed that he believed that Jesus was the Messiah. I could
write the words 'Jesus Christ is Lord' on a blackboard. That is a
statement, and to someone who could read only Chinese, it would
appear a strange jumble of scribbles! However, behind that statement is a truth, a profound truth, and nobody but God himself can
reveal that truth to me. That points to the main danger in having
religion as a subject in final exams in second-level schools. What a
travesty it would be if anyone confused religious knowledge, with
its facts and data about religious beliefs, with actual truths about
God, which can never be found in a book! When Jesus asks 'Who do
you say that I am?' I must go straight to my heart, and find my
answer to that question there. I may have the theological definitions
of Jesus as Saviour, Redeemer, Lord, and God, but, when I go down
into my heart I may not find those answers there. Instead I may find
guilt, fear, discouragement, and enough of emptiness to show me

that Jesus is certainly not any of those things for me. The kid at the end of the story in this reflection was right. When the priest had to resort to theological definitions from a text-book, rather than speak out of what he knew, through reflection and personal experience, then the kid was both sharp and very correct to say 'Sure he doesn't know either, sure he doesn't?'!

Heavenly Father, I know that we are your children. I like to think that, in your eyes, and as you see us, we actually are children. I trust your Spirit at work within to develop in me the heart of a child. The heart that trusts, that depends, that just knows that you have everything under control. I neither desire nor need to understand any great mysteries. Just to know you are there, and that you know I'm here, that's enough for me. Thank you, Father. Amen.

23. Learning to listen

It is generally accepted that creative listening generates creative sharing. Having someone prepared to listen is a priceless treasure. Listening is an art, and it is also a virtue. It is a wonderful way to compliment another, in that it confirms you in your sense of self-worth when another is prepared to listen to what you have to say. Listening is at the heart of prayer, which is always two-way. When I speak, God listens. I have his full attention. Knowing this can be a great help, as I pour out my soul, and speak from the heart. It becomes a problem, however, when my role is that of someone who is always talking, and God is expected to do all the listening! 'Listen, Lord, your servant is speaking' is far from being the prayer of the humble soul. Prayer is not so much me speaking to God who doesn't hear, as God speaking to me who may not listen. 'Speak, Lord, your servant is listening' is the proper attitude to bring to that space and time I give to God, which we call prayer.

As I write I am aware of a television set in the background. It is not switched on, of course, and so there's no picture. This does not mean that there are no pictures being transmitted from several studios. It means that the conditions are not present at this end for receiving those pictures. I am convinced that God is always communicating with his people, and only those who are tuned in are actually hearing what he is saying. God's word is an extraordinary gift, that has infinite power. 'Say but the word, and I shall be healed … At your word I will let down the net.' Jesus himself is a Word from God. Word here is much more than a unit in a dictionary. 'Did you get any word from Carol yet?' is asking if there is any message yet. Jesus is such a word from the Father. Through the work of the Spirit, the Father continues to speak a message of invitation, a message of hope, a message of love. They are happy and blessed, indeed, who have learned to listen to God's word. They are spiritu-

ally well-nourished, and have a constant sense of never being alone.
Of them it is said that they are never less alone than when alone.

To all intents and purposes, it was a typical family, father, mother,
three children. The father was a decent sort, even if a little rough
at the edges. He could be prodigally generous on one issue, and
be a real miser on something else. Somewhere in his mind, he
seemed to beat a drum, and if his children didn't seem to march
to the beat of that drum, they were told just how inadequate,
how unambitious, how hopeless they were. The mother was a
much more wholesome and balanced person, much more consistent, and dependable. She helped the children cope with
dad's crazy moments, and, generally, they seemed to get by.

One of the boys was a bit backward, a bit slow on the uptake, a
trifle hesitant in all his responses. For some extraordinary reason, he worshipped his father, and hungered and thirsted for
every sign and signal of approval. His father was not particularly
sensitive to this, or indeed, to the boy in general. One day, however, the boy was speechless, when his dad returned from work,
and handed him a walkman. The lad just sat there, with his
mouth open, unable to find words. His mother was his anchor,
so he jumped up, and ran straight to her, to tell what had happened. He came back to the front room, with his words of thanks
now at the ready. As he entered the room, his brother was going
out the front door, with the walkman on his belt, and the phones
on his head. The lad was shocked, and was particularly upset
when his dad explained what had happened. From the dad's
perspective, the young lad had left the walkman on the table,
walked away, and ignored it. The father interpreted that as
indifference, and so he gave it to his brother. Once again, the
father wasn't listening.

Words are often the weakest form of communication. If I am a person who wears some sort of invisible antennae on my head, I will
hear a great deal as I enter a room, even if no one is speaking. At a
grave-side, a squeeze of a hand, or an arm around a shoulder will
often say much more than many words. Some years ago a friend of
mine, in frustration, described how he experienced his weekly
prayer-group. 'There's one half who just sit there all night and say

nothing. Then there's the other half who talk all night, and say nothing'! We all come across someone from time to time, and the impression is that there is absolutely no connection between the tongue and the brain, as we are treated to a monologue of unrelated, unrelenting verbiage! It is usually true that such people don't make good listeners either!

To be a listener is to have a heart that is filled with compassion. In other words, I want to hear what you have to say because I care about you. This also presumes humility, because I give precedence to what you have to say over anything I might want to say. I'm sure we all have found ourselves waiting till the other paused for breath, so that we could jump in with a much more interesting story! From the time we were aware of what we had to say, the other person ceased to have a listener, as we waited to pounce. It is a very real form of humility, and a special expression of love, that we should be willing to put someone else in front of ourselves, when it comes to sharing ideas, problems, or experiences. Quite often, the only help the other needs is a sympathetic, listening ear. I certainly would not claim to be the world's greatest listener, but, on occasions, someone has thanked me sincerely for all my help, while all I had done was to sit and listen. In the category of ministries and services, there certainly should be one called 'listening'!

The image of a body is a simple and powerful way of expressing the reality of the church, or the Christian community. Each one of us is a member of that body. To form a body, we all need to be different, or we end up with all heads, or all hands! The ear is part of the body, and maybe it is significant that we have two of those, and only one tongue! The people in the community who express love and service through providing a listening, compassionate ear, are real jewels within the structure. They are life-giving people, in so far as such people infuse new life into others by the confirmation of their listening. A sure and certain sign that I have had a Pentecost is my ability to confirm others. The listeners are special Pentecost people, and they are always in the business of building up the church in love. They represent the listening heart of Jesus that is filled with love and compassion for others. Jesus it is who invites all the burdened and the weary to come to him, and to tell him all about it. His willingness and his ability to listen is what gives rest to the human spirit. Normally, it might be hoped that I would enter into such an encounter as the speaker, and end up as the listener. When I begin to become the listener I am on my way to recovery.

The father in the story was probably a good man, but he lacked something very basic, and very essential. His love of the other was not the love that accepts the other exactly where he/she is at, which is fundamental to all understanding of God's love for us. The boy spoke loudly and clearly when he received the gift, but, because he didn't use words, his father didn't hear him. One look at his face with the eyes of love, and he would have understood fully. Such people can be very destructive, even if, frequently, they do not intend to be. Just as the genuine listener develops the knack of listening without being fully conscious of doing so, so do some people succeed in hurting and destroying others, without being aware of what they're doing. 'Father, forgive them, they know not what they're doing' is a prayer that extends far beyond the confines of the crucifixion on Calvary.

Heavenly Father, I never ever think of you not listening! Thank you for that. I have to constantly trust your patience, your understanding, and your compassion, and I also have to remind myself that all of that is endless and limitless. What a consolation that is! Thanks, Father. I ask your Spirit to continue to reveal all the dimensions of your love, and to open my heart to the fulness of that love. Amen.

24. Discovering the pearl within

Life, as we now experience it, is a journey from one birth to another birth. It continues the process of gestation, until we finally become all that God has called us to be and has created us to be. Life is not about achievement, but, rather it is an end in itself. We are always in the process of becoming. When Jesus came that first time, he set the snowball rolling. When he comes at the end of time, he will complete the process, and will harvest the result of everything he has done. It is his work, and his work only, from beginning to end. Between both comings, in the meantime, Jesus continues to come to us every moment of every day, if we are but open to that. The door of our heart has but one handle, and that is on the inside. He comes to us just as we are, and it is never necessary that I be anything other than what he sees when he looks at me. He enters our hearts through the cracks of our brokenness. During that in-between time ('as we wait in joyful hope for the coming of our Saviour, Jesus Christ') we are caught in the tensions of struggle, and of dealing with the push and pull of living. Wholeness is about being open to reconciliation within my heart, where the good, the bad, and the ugly are recognised and acknowledged. It is about shaking free from the clutches of denial, and being willing to name, claim, and tame my demons. I am every single person in the gospels. Within my spirit I can find the prodigal son and his self-righteous brother, the Pharisee and the publican, Martha and Mary. Reconciliation is about mutual acceptance of both sides of the coin within, about making friends with my shadow. If I am ever to be redeemed and freed from bondage, then I must be willing to be totally available to the Lord. This involves throwing the door wide open, inviting God in, and giving him total freedom to effect his will in me. This is so much more radical than picking out this, that, and the other, and asking God to make them right. When I was growing up, we did something like that, and we called it Confession! If I am honest, I have no reason to trust myself, because I can easily be very selective in what I decide the Lord should do for me, and in me. His plans for my welfare could be so much different from my own.

The first stage of life is the womb-life. Life, once begun, never ends, but it continues to develop through many stages of evolution. The gestation period is a direct preparation for the next stage of life, and when the baby reaches a certain level of viability, it then moves on to the second stage of life. During that period of gestation, it is not unusual to discover that, among other things, the baby has developed a remarkable resemblance to one or both parents. In a physical sense the baby has been formed in the image and likeness of its parents. The second stage of life is like being in the womb of God, where I am being formed in the image and likeness of his Son, Jesus Christ. Christianity is about becoming Christ-like, and a Christian is someone who is open to becoming another Christ. This is not, now or ever, something that we ourselves can do. It is the work of God's Spirit, the Spirit that came upon Mary, so that Jesus assumed flesh within her. Once the baby has been born into the Christian family, the next part of the plan is an initiation ceremony into the family of God, which we call Baptism. This is best understood when we consider the process of adoption. The baby has natural, biological parents, but for some good reason, outside of their control, they find that they have to hand the baby over to a new set of parents, who will take full responsibility for the baby from now on, even to giving the baby full legal access to their home, their name, and everything that they are. As the baby grows up within the family of adoption it is not unusual to notice a family resemblance developing, as the child takes on the personal habits, characteristics, and attitudes of the adoptive parents. In the same way, after many years of adoption into the family of God, through Baptism, it is to be hoped that some kind of family resemblance begins to emerge. The image of God is stamped on the spirit, and time should permit that to emerge into external evidence.

The young lad was on his way to school. As he passed the sculptor's yard, he noticed a huge block of marble on a stand, and the sculptor was getting ready to begin a new project. The young lad had to continue on his way, and he was disappointed to discover that the front doors of the sculptor's workshop were closed every day after that, as he passed by on his way to and from school. Each day, however, as he passed, he could hear the sound of chisel and hammer, and he knew that the work was progressing. He longed for the day when the front doors would be open again, and his curiosity would be satisfied by discovering what the task in hand was.

The great day finally arrived. One morning, on his way to school, he found the front doors open, and he certainly needed no invitation to wander in for a look. He was awe-struck to discover that where the original block of marble had been, there now was a figure of a tiger, huge, menacing, and very life-like. The lad continued to stare at this for some moments, in total amazement. Then he turned to the sculptor, and, in total innocence, asked 'Excuse me, sir, but … but … but how did you know there was a tiger in there?'!

When God looks at us, he knows 'what's in there'. One of the surest ways of bringing out that inner image is to surround me in life by all the people who will contribute to the revelation of what is within. These people can combine the iron fist and the velvet glove. Some of the personalities are like silk, and others are like sandpaper! This person will make me very patient, while that other person will make me a good listener! God has strange ways of making us holy! Ideally, it would be a wonderful grace to stand up amidst the situations, circumstances, and people of my life, and say 'Yes', and bloom where I'm planted! On a human level, of course, this is not possible, because human nature is volatile, and can never be relied on. I try not to use 'big' words (!), but I would like to use the word 'mercurial' here, because, to me, it gives a fairly accurate idea of how I see human nature. Mercury is of such a substance that it is impossible to pick up a drop of mercury between the fingers. It runs all over the place, and it divides and sub-divides into many smaller particles. Human nature is not easy to manipulate or to manage, and it is entirely unpredictable. Only God is constant. I can start out with the best intentions in the world, but, by myself, I just cannot sustain such a commitment. Because I am human, I am always in a condition of change. Life is a dynamic, it is never static. If it is not moving forward, it is moving backwards.

Life is a process, rather than actually becoming anything, or arriving anywhere. I never become a Christian, but I'm always in the process of becoming. I continue to say 'yes', and to make myself available to the process. I continue to 'show up', as it were, and I trust and expect that the miracle will happen! I speak of pure miracle here, something that only God can do. There are two conditions for most miracles in the gospel. Firstly, the person concerned has done everything possible, and, at long last, is convinced beyond all doubt that 'whatever I'm doing is not working'! Jairus did all he could for his daughter, the centurion did all he could for his servant, but all to no avail. The little woman in the crowd had spent all her money over the previous twelve years on doctors bills, the man at the pool had waited for thirty-eight years in the hope of being healed, and Peter had fished all night without success. The second condition is represented by the words 'If I can touch the hem of his garment I will be healed … Say but the word and my servant will be healed … At your word I will let down the net.'

Revelation is an important and very significant word in the whole process of spirituality. It implies something that is already there being revealed or drawn to our attention. The real me, that part made in the image and likeness of God, is always there, but it takes a whole life of chipping and refining to reveal the treasure within. There is an eastern religion that speaks of the real self being a pearl in muddy water, and only when I become still for some length of time, and the muddy water settles, can I begin to see the pearl within. That makes a very meaningful image of what real prayer is about, where God's revelation of himself, and of ourselves, are made possible. God knows what is within us, and he would love us to know it also.

> *Holy Spirit, Spirit and Breath of God, I look to you as the one who reveals, the one who forms, the one who moulds. It is uniquely your work to bring forth the inner life and power invested in me, as a Christian. Melt me, mould me, fill me, use me. Spirit of the Living God, fall afresh on me. Amen.*

25. Bloom where you're planted

I'm sure the following scenario has repeated itself many many times. A Religious Sister, in a nursing or teaching Congregation, rings the door bell of an enclosed convent of Sisters, and announces that she is interested in entering there. So far so good, and all very laudable. During the process that follows, it must be clearly established why Sister wishes to join an enclosed community, and, specifically, this particular one. More than likely, it is because she feels drawn to the contemplative life, and that is understandable, and is a special grace given to people whom the Lord chooses. On the other hand, if it is discovered that Sister wishes to enter this community because she wants to become holy, then I would hope her request would no longer be entertained! Holiness is a funny thing! It is not something we do, rather is it something that happens to us. A baby will get hair, teeth, and nails, but there is nothing can be done to hurry up the process. Holiness is a form of gestation. It is a process of change, of evolution, and it is expected that the person concerned would be the very last to notice it! (If the reverse be true, then we can question the outcome!) It would be wrong to think of the Trinity, Father, Son, and Spirit, as having distinctly different roles, which are mutually exclusive. Ice, snow, and hail-stones is still water, no matter what form it takes. In a general way, however, it helps us understand if we think of Jesus as saving us (forgiveness, redemption, freedom from bondage), and the Spirit as making us holy (sanctifying, anointing, empowering). The Father initiated the work (by sending Jesus), Jesus carries out the first major part of the plan (redemption), and the Spirit completes the work (personalising all of that within each of us). All members of the Trinity are involved in our salvation. Because of the nature of God, there is no way we can compartmentalise that nature, or exclude any part from the activity of the whole. In other words, I cannot speak of a bit of God here, a part of God there, or some element of God being involved somewhere else. Human language is as limited as the person using it, and nowhere is language so limited as when we speak of God. The image of a triangle, with the Father at the top, the Son at the left bottom corner, and the Spirit at the right bottom corner, all of that is but a futile human attempt to present to the human mind something that is infinite, and incapable of definition. I believe, however, that we should continue our attempts, albeit futile, to image God in various ways. The ultimate goal, of course, is that we come into full possession of the final promises of Jesus at the Last Supper, when he said that 'We will come and make our abode ...'

The idea of becoming a Holy of Holies is an awesome thought, but it is exactly what Jesus had in mind. The human heart is destined to become a Pentecost place, a house of prayer, a place of the Spirit, where the Father, the Son, and the Spirit make their abode. If I call this a place of the Spirit, I do so simply to stress that making this possible is directly the work of the Spirit, who brings us the fulness of grace. Because of Incarnation, God has come so close to us as to be part of what we are, and, therefore, it is that much more difficult for us to notice him! It is not possible to 'stand back' for an objective view of God! I often think of myself as a tiny fish out in the midst of the Atlantic, swimming around, gaining new experiences of the same sea, but being totally unable to rise up above the water, and get an over-all view from coast to coast. (I would be a very foolish little fish, and a very dead little fish, if I tried that!) Like a baby in the womb, I am in a sustaining sack that helps to develop and nurture me to completion.

A young lad had been reading some of the lives of the Saints, and he came to the conclusion that he, too, would like to be a saint. He decided to give this some thought, because he needed to decide what kind of saint he was going to be. He had read of Simon Stylites, who lived on a pillar down in the town square, and he thought that this was a very good idea, because if he was going to be a saint he might as well get maximum publicity for the effort! He didn't have a pillar to climb up on, so he decided to begin on a much smaller scale. He got a chair in the kitchen, and he stood up in it! After a while his sister came in the side door, and nearly knocked him down. He moved away from the door, only to be told by his mother that she couldn't get to the fridge, because he was in the way! He moved elsewhere, and within a short while his dad came in from the sitting-room, bumped into him, and actually knocked him and his chair. This was too much for our brave saint-to-be, who pushed the chair to one side, walked out the door, and declared 'No, it's not possible! It's just not possible to become a saint at home'!

The basic truth behind everything I am saying in this section is that it is not possible to become a saint anywhere else! Wherever I'm living right now has everything necessary to make me holy. The action takes place within, and the more that happens there, the more life-giving becomes the reaction that comes from within. In life, the miles stretch ahead of me, but the things that mess up my life are within me. God works from the inside out. To fully accept the presence of God within, which results from my Baptism, is to expect that inner Presence to come back out again, through the words I say, and the things I do. It is only God who makes people, places, and things holy. If God is present in them, they are holy, if he is absent, they are not holy. Of all the sacred shrines throughout the world, of all the places that have been made sacred because of some divine intervention, the human heart is God's favoured and favourite place of dwelling. Jesus told the woman at the well that the day would come when we would worship God in spirit and in truth, and that could never be confined to the Temple, or to some holy mountain. In mentioning both the Temple and the holy mountain, Jesus was speaking to Jew and Samaritan alike, because each excluded the possibility of the other having a place that might possibly be as special as their own. I grew up in a church that told me that outside this church there was no salvation! Nobody would defend that now, but it is frightening to think that just a few years ago, this was church teaching. Only God can do God-things! Redemption, salvation, and sanctification are uniquely divine undertakings! My contribution is my willingness to make myself available.

The prevalent sin is when we turn the divine initiative into human endeavour; when we highjack an idea of God's, make it our own, act as if the idea had come from us, and attempt to do things our way. It doesn't take much reflection to identify this as just another version of original sin, the sin of Adam and Eve dressed up in modern clothes. I am not at all advocating some form of passivism, where I do nothing, and expect God to do everything. (Like the man whose beard went on fire, and he prayed that it might start raining!) My input is very definite, and centrally important. When Jesus went back to Nazareth, he couldn't work any miracles there, because of their lack of faith. In other words, because of God's scrupulous respect for our free-will, his freedom to work in and through us is determined by our willingness to allow him do so. If I go out the front door, after a shower of rain, there is one thing that is usually very obvious. Some parts of the ground are quite dry, while other parts are covered in pools of water. It was the same amount of rain that fell on all parts. The difference is that one part of the ground is packed tight, hard, and closed, and the water cannot enter. The other part is loose, open, porous, and welcoming, and the water enters in without any problem. People are like that! I can become a saint anywhere, if I allow God have his way with me. 'Lord, help me believe that nothing ever happens me in life that is not seen by you as something that is necessary for my spiritual growth and welfare.' That's a brave prayer, and the prayer of a faith that is trusting and complete ...

Holy Spirit, Breath of God, I ask you, please, to anoint me. Anoint me with the blessing of wholeness, with an open heart, with a generous spirit. Please create a new heart in me, and put a steadfast spirit within me. Firm up my weaknesses, shore up my brokenness, and bandage up my wounds. May I know your presence, your blessing, and your anointing. Amen.

26. Almost a saint

I must confess that, for many years of my life, my idea of a saint was someone who was so heavenly as to be no earthly good! I even thought that, to be a saint, one had to be skinny! (I knew nothing of Thomas Aquinas at the time!) I had seen these pictures of gaunt ascetic-looking creatures, badly in need of something to eat. What made the picture more off-putting was that some of them had a skeleton on the desk, had an arrow through the heart, or holes in the palms of the hands. This, certainly wasn't for me! Becoming a saint, or being a saint, was certainly not for the faint-hearted! This was 'Onward Christian Soldiers' right to the last drop of blood.

I remember being puzzled when I first read where St Paul sends greetings and love 'to all the saints at Antioch.' That seemed to be slightly over the top! Thank God, in time, I came to understand that any person or any place in which God lives is holy, is sanctified. Anybody who is sanctified through the presence of God's indwelling Spirit is a saint. My confusion and misunderstanding came from our use of the word 'canonised', which, of course, is not at all a necessity or a pre-requisite. I was at an ordination of a friend and colleague some months ago. The whole ceremony was very meaningful, and well thought out. The presiding bishop had the great gift of never seeming to get in the way. This was obviously a ritual of commitment between this young man, his God, and God's people. Many people from the parish in which he had spent his dia-conate year were directly involved in the ceremony at different stages. His mother helped vest him for the Mass, and many of the laity present joined with the priests in laying hands of blessing upon him. One of the abiding memories I have, in what was a truly memorable ceremony, was the Litany of the Saints. I had always thought of this as being fairly heavy going, and I resigned myself to put down my head, and see this through! Imagine my surprise (and my delight) when I heard the saints being invoked. Very few of

them are canonised, and more than half were not Catholic! Steve
Biko, Martin Luther King, Mahatma Ghandi, etc., etc. The list went
on and on, and my heart was singing! Instead of the seemingly endless saint after saint I had expected, most of whom were from so far
back that it would be legitimate to question if they had ever existed,
I was hearing names of people who shared and shaped this world
during my own life-time, and who certainly held a place of respect,
awe, and reverence in my own heart. This was one time when I
wished the Litany of the Saints would keep going, and I was disappointed when it ended.

> In *The Power and the Glory*, Graham Greene tells of a priest who
> was condemned to death during an era of religious persecution
> in Mexico. The terrifying tensions in his life in recent years had
> driven him to drink. It was the morning of his death. He
> crouched on the floor of his cell, with an empty brandy flask in
> his hand, trying to remember the words of the Act of Contrition.
> He was confused. It was not the good death for which he had
> always prayed. What a fool he had been to think that he could
> have stayed, while others had fled! 'What an impossible fellow I
> am', he thought. 'I've never done anything worthwhile for any-
> body. I might as well never have lived.' Tears poured down his
> cheeks. He was not, at that moment, afraid of damnation. He felt
> only an immense disappointment, because he now had to go to
> God empty-handed. It seemed to him, right then, that it would
> have been quite easy to have been a saint. All it would have
> required was a little courage, and a little self-restraint. He felt
> like someone who had missed happiness by seconds, at an
> appointed place. He knew now that, at the end, there was only
> one thing that counted, – to be a saint.

I remember, as I read that, feeling enormous empathy, support, and
love for the tortured soul at that moment. To me, he was a saint, but
not anything like how he had envisioned sainthood. The one thing
that bothered me was that he seemed to have lost hope, and I
always considered that to be the only real sin a Christian can commit. In the story, he died as a result of his commitment, and, I convinced myself, he then discovered that holiness has little to do with
perfection. Only God is perfect. The saint is a sinner who kept trying, and who received the blessings in store for those of good-will.

Everything is gift, and heaven is God's greatest and eternal gift. Our glory consists not in never falling, but in getting up every time we fall. To continue to try, is heaven, and to stay down when we fall is hell. What struck me most, and what lasted longest in my memory, was the deep conviction that all was well with him, no matter how he himself felt. This challenged me about the times, in my own life, when I myself had been so out of touch with God's love and acceptance, that I allowed myself to feel outside of the parameters of that same love and acceptance. I experienced a much greater empathy and acceptance of his position than I had ever extended to myself when I was experiencing alienation from God, and from everything that is good. It may sound foolish, at least, and presumptuous, at best, when I say that, if I were God, I would rejoice in welcoming this troubled soul into eternal bliss and happiness.

There is a wonderful description in Matthew's gospel (chapter 25) of the general judgement. Those who are invited to enter into eternal glory are the most surprised people you could imagine! They just cannot account for how they could have qualified! 'When did we see you hungry, thirsty, naked, or in prison?' Their doing and giving was so ordinary that they never thought of this leading to eternal reward. They probably thought that it would surely require something very exceptional and extraordinary to merit such a reward. Obviously, their starting-point was their own weakness, and, with this, they could have no great hopes! They had forgotten or misunderstood the words of Jesus, when he said, again and again, that he had come looking for the lost, the outcast, the helpless, and the hopeless. Heaven is God's last laugh, because, no matter how we try to rationalise his plan of salvation to fit into our way of seeing and doing things, it is going to be his way in the end! There are three things that may surprise you when you get to heaven. You will be surprised at some of the people you will see there! You will be surprised at some of the people who may not be there! And you will be totally surprised to find yourself there! (If you are surprised at some of the people you see there, please check the place out, because, with such a judgement, you may not be in heaven at all!)

Life is not about achievement. It is not about accomplishing. It is about plodding ahead, continually opening my heart to the gift of every new day. The result and outcome of all this is totally up to

God. When I take responsibility for the outcome, I have begun to play God, and that is original sin in its worst form. God becomes God in my life the very moment I stop playing God. Again and again we are faced with the struggle between what God wants to do for us, and how we want him to do it! It may sound very simple, but, because of our damaged human condition, because of original sin, there is only one way in which this can all happen: Let go and let God. Only God can do God things, and becoming holy, and entering heaven, where we can spend an eternity in God's presence, is something that God thought of in the first place, and only his Spirit can accomplish. If we could only be open to God's way of doing things, we would all end up as saints, skinny or not!

Lord Jesus, I can fully identify with the priest in the story. I sometimes feel myself before you with empty hands. I ask you, Lord, please, to fill my hands and my heart with your love. I pray that your Spirit might continue to reveal the truth to me. Is it part of your truth, Lord, that the filling comes from you, and what I supply is the emptiness? Thank you, Lord. Amen.

27. Living in the Kingdom

There are three kingdoms, the kingdom of God, the kingdom of this world, and the kingdom of Satan. Each kingdom has very different values and priorities. The kingdoms of Satan and of the world, however, are happy bed-fellows, because they share a lot in their common qualities. (I realise that I have included the remainder of this paragraph in a previous Reflection. This is not an oversight, or yet another sign of approaching senility! It comes from my own personal conviction that this is something we should hear every day). If we go to the last book in the Bible (Revelations), and read chapter twelve, we get some idea how both the kingdom of Satan and the kingdom of the world are tied in together. There was war in heaven, and Lucifer (Satan) was expelled, and cast down to earth. This phrase is repeated four times in the same chapter. It is a mistake to think of Satan as being in hell. He is alive and well, and living on this planet earth. A casual glance at the daily papers, or listening to the news headlines, on radio or TV, would give evidence to the reality of that fact. When Jesus came, he called Satan 'the prince of this world'. Satan took Jesus up on a high mountain, and offered him the kingdom of this world if he would bow down and adore him. Let's not forget that the kingdom of this world was Satan's to give. Jesus came across a man who was possessed by so many demons that they said their name was Legion. They begged Jesus not to send them down into the abyss, and so he allowed them enter a herd of pigs. The implication here is that the time for sending Satan 'the rest of the way', as it were, has not yet come. That will happen when Jesus returns in triumph at the end of time. The kingdom of this world, with its false gods and wrong priorities, will come to an end, and the kingdom of Satan on this earth will end, when Satan is sent the rest of the way, the gates of hell are closed forever, and Satan can no longer seek to thwart any of God's plans, or harm any of God's people.

Jesus made it very clear, again and again, that his kingdom was not of this world. It was in the world, certainly, but it did not belong to this world. All its values and qualities are totally opposed to the values of this world. People with a worldly mind-set could not possibly understand what Jesus spoke of. They could understand only worldly things, and the kingdom of Jesus was not one of those. St John wrote that the fact that his readers wanted to hear God's word was proof positive that they were of God, because people of the world would not want to listen, or to hear. The witness of the presence of God's kingdom on earth is given by those who live according to the rules of that kingdom. Such people are precious in God's eyes, because they help make the gospel credible. They are many many aspects of the gospel message that I came to accept and believe because I came across someone who gave witness to them.

Once a village blacksmith had a vision. An angel of the Lord came to him and said 'The Lord has sent me. The time has come for you to take up your place in his kingdom.' 'I thank God for thinking of me,' said the blacksmith, 'but, as you know, the season for sowing the crops will soon be here. The people of the village will need their ploughs repaired, and their horses shod. I don't wish to seem ungrateful, but do you think I might put off taking my place in the kingdom until I have finished?' The angel looked at him in the wise and loving way of angels. 'I'll see what can be done', he said, and he vanished. The blacksmith continued with his work, and was almost finished, when he heard of a neighbour who fell ill right in the middle of the planting season. The next time he saw the angel, the blacksmith pointed towards the barren fields, and pleaded with the angel 'Do you think eternity can hold off a little longer? If I don't finish this job, my friend's family will suffer.' Again, the angel smiled, and vanished. The blacksmith's friend recovered, but another's barn burned down, and a third was deep in sorrow at the death of his wife. And the fourth ... and so on. Whenever the angel reappeared, the blacksmith just spread out his hands in a gesture of resignation and compassion, and drew the angel's eyes to where the suffering was.

One evening, the blacksmith began to think of the angel, and how he'd put him off for such a long time. He felt very old and

tired, and he prayed 'Lord, if you would like to send your angel
again, I think I would like to see him now.' He'd no sooner spoken than the angel stood before him. 'If you still want to take
me', said the blacksmith, 'I am now ready to take my place in the
kingdom of the Lord.' The angel looked at the blacksmith, and
smiled, as he said 'Where do you think you have been all these
years?

There are three simple rules that govern life in the kingdom of God.
In the world, my god can be money, power, pleasure, or self-will. In
God's kingdom, Jesus is Lord, and what he says is what determines
my actions. In the kingdom of this world, people are viewed in
terms of usefulness, wealth, influence, or power. In the kingdom of
God, the most handicapped child is on this earth with as much right
as the greatest genius that ever lived. In the kingdom of this world,
I can get my power from political, social, or financial clout. In the
kingdom of God, all of the power is freely supplied by God, and
this is the Person called the Holy Spirit. It is evident, then, that both
kingdoms are diametrically opposed to each other in every possible
way.

Pilate asked Jesus 'Are you a king, then?', to which Jesus replied
'Yes, I am a king, and it is for this reason that I have come. My kingdom, however, is not of this world; otherwise some earthly power
would attempt to rescue me, and prevent you having your will
with me. But my kingdom is not of this world.' Later, because of a
total inability to grasp the truth of what Jesus had proclaimed, the
soldiers mocked him as a king of fools, with a cloak of mockery, a
sceptre of a clown, and a crown of thorns. Only someone like the
blacksmith in our story could recognise the King of Kings in the
guise of what the world considered a subject of scorn and disdain.

People like the blacksmith have a tough time in this world! They are
seen as misfits, because, in truth, they certainly do not fit into what
the world considers important. They are intrusions, like folks from
another planet, and they just refuse to conform, and 'become like
the rest of us.' Members of God's kingdom are different. They are a
sign, but a sign of contradiction. They speak of other values, they
speak another language, they draw the ire, anger, and scorn of the
world, because they touch us at a level which we might prefer to

deny, and they become our conscience. I can do amazing things to my own conscience, but, when that comes from someone else, I am not in control, and that provokes aggression, anger, and a compulsion to annihilate. The Martin Luther Kings and the Mahatma Ghandis of this world just had to be killed, because that was preferable to having to listen to what they had to say. Killing the messenger, however, just because I don't like the message, is something that is as old as the human race. I might be highly offended if someone told me I was insane! However, if I am honest, when it comes to the basic truths of this present reflection, I can certainly be guilty of very insane behaviour! There is some sort of stubborn rebelliousness deep within us that is determined to fight God all the way, and to insist on doing things our way. As Jesus dressed as a slave, and washed the apostles' feet, he spoke of such service as being the hallmark of being great in his kingdom. That is certainly a 'turn-up' for the books!

Lord Jesus, I want to live in your kingdom. I desire and ask that your Spirit might inspire within me a sense of service, and a spirit of generosity. Please use me, Lord, in any way you wish in the building up of your kingdom. I can only declare my willingness and availability, and I trust you, Lord, to take it from there. I am more than willing to move, but only if you lead the way. I have every reason to believe that you are more than willing to lead. Thank you, Lord. Amen.

28. The unknown God

In most major capitals around the world there is a place of reverence and pilgrimage known as the Grave of the Unknown Soldier. This serves as a sort of cover-all for all the soldiers who died in battle, and whose names are not inscribed on a tombstone. By the very fact that we have such places of remembrance, it shows some sort of desire on our part to remember the nameless and the un-numbered ones, and, I would hope, this is more than just us trying to take care of our guilt. 'Let's build a monument to 'all the others', and that will take care of them, and help us feel better.' In the Acts of the Apostles (chapter 17) we read of Paul's visit to Athens. 'As I walked around, looking at your shrines, I even discovered an altar inscribed: To an unknown God.' Paul then proceeds to explain to them who this unknown God is, and, after a very long dissertation, in which he makes some strong and cogent arguments for accepting the God of the New Testament, he is met by a reply which must be the bane of all preachers, 'That's very interesting. We must hear him again sometime'! In other words, there is nothing going to be done now. Some other time …

God is more than willing to reveal himself to anyone who wants to know him. Flesh and blood does not, or cannot, reveal this. Jesus said 'Nobody knows the Father except the Son, and those to whom the Son chooses to reveal him.' If I drew a circle, and made that represent the parameters of my knowledge, then God, who is infinite, cannot possibly be contained within that circle. There is no way I can know God, even if, through personal encounters, I can experience dimensions of God. God is continually in some process of self-revelation, and he is always more than willing to lead us into an ever-deeper consciousness of who and what he is. I often think of God on stand-by, as it were, awaiting the O.K. from me, so that he can move, and do in, with, for, and through me what his great love would dearly wish to do.

Upon a mountain-top there lived a kind and gentle God. In the village, far below, his people lived. They were a very busy people, with many books to read, many games to play, and many meetings to attend. They seldom thought about the kind and gentle God, so far away did he seem. No one had even seen his face. Some doubted he was even there at all.

Yet, day by day, the gentle God looked down upon his own, and wanted very much that they should be his friends. 'I must' he thought, 'do some small thing to show them that I care.' And so, each day he sent a messenger to the village, a pack upon his back, and in the pack there was a special gift for everyone in the village.

Each day the gifts arrived. Each day the people ran with open arms to gather them. Soon, however, they grew quite used to being gifted. Some began to grab gifts from the pack, some took more than they were meant to have, and some complained of gifts that were too small. Far up on his mountain sat God. Day after lonely day he waited for a friendly word, a sign of thanks, or just a 'Hi, God. I know you're there.' But no word came. The people took the gifts as if they had a right to them, and more. God? Well, he was far away. And some said 'What has he ever done for me?' And others 'I don't believe he even exists.'

'If I can't tell them that I am,' God thought, 'how can I tell them that I am a friend, and that I want to give them friendship most of all?' And then his eyes lit up. 'I know', he said, 'I'll give a party for my friends below. I'll give a party, and I'll invite them all. Surely if they spend some time with me, and learn to known how much I really care, oh, surely they'll come to know I am their friend.' And so the invitations were sent out. A list was posted on the town hall door, so that all could come and put a tick after a name, to indicate a willingness to accept the invitation. Some just laughed, and said 'That's not for me!' And some said 'Spend a day with God? No way!' And some were very busy with their chores, and said 'Some other time, but not today.' Some were tempted. 'Maybe it is for real, and maybe God does want to be my friend.' Timidly, they signed up for the day. But when others laughed, they were ashamed, and soon found excuses why they couldn't go.

The party day arrived, but no one went. And in his mountain home the kind God sat. 'I only want to give them love', he said. 'How can I tell them? Make them understand? Is there no one who wants me for a friend?' And in the village far below, the people laughed and cried; they worked and played and died. And seldom, if ever, did they think about the gentle God who loved them very much.

The average person walking down the road believes in God, but may not be too sure that he/she needs God right now! This parable 'limps' in places, in that it is not true that God lives on the top of some remote mountain! For many people, there may be no sense of immanence or nearness about God, but it would be wrong to believe that this is God's fault. I remember seeing a poster one time, and there was a cat lying down, looking sad, and looking straight ahead. On the poster were the words 'Does God seem far away? Guess who moved?!' In the spirituality propounded in Twelve Step programmes for alcohol, drug and food addiction, etc., they speak of God 'as we understand him'. In simple English, when I examine what my understanding of God is, and how I conceptualise God, then I could do myself a great big favour by getting rid of the God I have! He may not be a God of love, and he just might live on the top of some remote mountain. As Christians, we believe in Incarnation, where God comes to live in us, and to take on the very nature, personality, and human being that I am. He will not do this, of course, unless I allow this happen. In a way, you know, God is wherever I say he is! If I say he is on the top of a remote mountain, then, effectively, that's where he is, as far as I am concerned!

This parable reminds us of how we can take God's gifts for granted. God's greatest gift is his Son Jesus. Jesus tells the story of a king who sent several messengers to negotiate a truce with a group of people. Each messenger was rejected, beaten up, and seriously injured. The king decided to send his own son, in the hope that they would surely respect him. However, so determined were they not to enter into some peaceful treaty with the king, that they actually killed the son. In another story, Jesus speaks of a rich man who died and ended up in hell. From there, he saw a poor man he had known, who was now in heaven. The rich man wanted to warn his brothers to avoid the fate that befell him, and he asked God to let him return to warn his brothers. He was told that they had the word of God and the prophets, and they should listen to that. The rich man argued that if he returned to them from the dead, they would surely listen, but God told him that if they refused to listen to what had already been said, they certainly would not pay any attention to someone coming back from the dead! Maybe the irony in this was lost on his hearers, but Jesus was being prophetic, because he was sure that, even after he himself came back from the dead, he would encounter the same excuses, the same rationalisation, the same indifference. Whether we know God or not is one question. It is obvious, however, when we listen to the stories and parables of Jesus that he certainly knows us!

Lord Jesus, I remember your words: This is eternal life, to know you, the one eternal God, and Jesus Christ, whom you have sent. Jesus, thank you for coming to reveal the Father to us. Thank you for a very clear and definite message. I turn to your Spirit again and again, because, with my human mind, even your simple message gets very complicated! Please don't give up on me, Lord! Thank you. Amen.

29. Carried by the Lord

Life is a journey. It is a journey from one birth to yet another birth. The Bible speaks of Adam and Eve being banished from the Garden, and, for us Christians, life is a journey back to the Garden. The first part of the Bible, the Old Testament, speaks of many and varied journeys. The most famous one is the journey from exile in Egypt, back to the Promised Land. This is the one that most accurately foreshadows our own life's journey. Moses was the forerunner of Jesus, the one who leads us back home. Jesus goes so far as to say that no one returns to the Father except through him. He is the gate, the door to the sheepfold, and no one enters by any other way.

The decision of God to join us on our journey, and to share that journey with us, in his Son Jesus, is what we call Incarnation. To fully grasp the ramifications of that must be an extraordinary gift indeed. I say 'must be', because I don't think any of us can have an idea just how much or how little of this we have made our own. It is so much beyond the limits of a mere human brain, that none of us can possibly have anything but a partial glimpse of what, effectively, is a mystery. Of course, I can experience much, and many things in the heart, that I can never hope to understand in the head. I personally believe that when I'm most in touch with my raw humanity, with all its limitations, brokenness, sinfulness, and powerlessness, and when I then invite Jesus right into that mess, to take over there, to lift me out of the quicksand, … it is at such a time that I am most likely to actually experience the reality of Incarnation on a personal level. The more I am convinced of my need for Jesus, through experiencing the sharp edges of my own brokenness, the more likely I am to experience and know his presence. Jesus was with the apostles in the boat, and he was asleep. Obviously, they were happy enough to let him sleep. When the storm blew up, however, and they were in imminent danger of sinking, they soon woke him up, and they were more than ready for a miracle. Up till that time they didn't need a miracle, because they were doing very well on their own. Nothing like an emergency to concentrate the mind!

It is important, of course, that I realise that Jesus travels with me on the journey anyhow, whether I'm aware of it, open to it, or availing of that fact. The bulb in the clay continues to be cared for, even if it's not growing. During the frost of winter, when nothing seems to be happening, the clay continues to protect, and provide what is needed. Even when the little child is in play-school, the mother at home continues to think, to love, to knit, to sew, and to cook, and the child continues to be central to all that she does. Even when I forget God, he never forgets me. 'I will never forget you, my people. I have carved you on the palm of my hand. I will never forget you, I will not leave you orphans, I will never forget my own.'

> One night a man had a dream. He dreamt he was walking along the beach with the Lord. Across the sky flashed scenes from his life. For each scene he noticed two sets of footprints in the sand; one belonged to him, the other to the Lord. When the last scene of his life flashed before him, he looked back at the footprints in the sand. He noticed that many times along the path of his life there was only one set of footprints. He also noticed that it happened at the saddest and lowest times of his life.

> This really bothered him, and he questioned the Lord about it. 'Lord, you said that once I decided to follow you, you'd walk with me all the way. But I have noticed that during the most troublesome times in my life, there's only one set of footprints. I don't understand why, when I needed you most, you would leave me.' The Lord replied 'My precious, precious child, I love you, and I would never leave you. During your times of trial and suffering, when you see only one set of footprints, it was then that I carried you.'

Hindsight is a great thing, and most of us have perfect vision at such times! In the US, this is sometimes called 'Monday-morning-quarter-backing', when we discover on Monday morning how we could have won the game on Sunday! The greatest hindsight of all, of course, must be to look back at this stage of life when I reach the third and final stage of the journey. I like to think that everything the Lord allowed happen to me in life had a potential for good in it, and may even have been necessary for my spiritual growth, whether it looked like that at the time or not. This could well include the time and circumstances of my death. Is it possible that, if I believed in coincidences, I would have to stop believing in God? Maybe coincidences are God's way of preserving his anonymity! We can be sure that God is never very far away, and, as the old Irish idiom says, his help is nearer than the door.

Human nature is always subject to change, just as the bodily system continues to wear and to renew itself. Only God is consistent, the same yesterday, today, and always. This latter truth is at the heart of the legend or parable under review. No matter whether I'm aware of it or not, or whether I am open to it or not, God continues to be there for me with total and consistent loyalty. I have every reason to have confidence, and to be reassured, and this can never come from myself, from anything I am, or from anything I do. After Jesus himself, the most perfect human being that ever walked on this earth was Mary. In her we see that extraordinary combination of basics that produces the ideal. She was so open to truth that she could not possibly believe a lie, or fall for a lie. Therefore, with total clear vision, she saw that, of herself, she was nothing, and was incapable of doing anything outside the parameters of her human nature. With equal clarity, she saw and believed that God could and does do all things. He does this wherever he so wishes, and wherever he is given the freedom. She was more than willing to give God a free hand within her, and, therefore, she was not at all surprised that extraordinary things should happen. Her Magnificat was a song of pure praise and of pure wonder. She magnified the Lord. Note the word magnify. The bigger your God, the smaller your problems. Some people have very big problems, because their god is far too small! 'If God is with us, who can be against us? ... Unless the Lord build the house, in vain do the builders labour.'

Having Jesus there to pick me up and carry me when the going gets tough is more than just a nice pious thought, or a consoling truth. It is a veritable life-preserver, because, without him being there, I never could make it on my own. It is a simple and basic fact of the spiritual life that salvation and redemption are pure gift, and nothing can be done, on a human level to merit or earn this. It isn't a matter of me half-saving my soul, and then letting Jesus finish off the job, or Jesus getting the process in motion, and I taking over to complete the task. From beginning to end, this is pure free gift. I can facilitate it, of course, and, indeed, I can hinder it. God never acts without due respect for my free will, and so he involves my willingness or non-willingness in every stage of his plans for me. Once again, I say that he doesn't give me anything, he offers me everything. The choice is always mine. The very fact of his grace being gift implies that I must have total freedom to accept or reject, otherwise it certainly would lack the basic quality of gift, if it contained an element of compulsion. As in the story of the footprints, God's help was so unobstructive that it even went unnoticed. Jesus describes the surprise of the good people at the general judgement, who exclaimed 'Lord, when did we ever do all those things you spoke of?' Doing good in such a way is the ideal level of love and selflessness combined, where doing the good is seen to be an end in itself.

> Lord Jesus, with all my heart I thank you for being there for me, through thick and thin. I just know you were there, when I look back and see how I survived particular storms. I know I'm not always aware of your presence, and I'm surely never grateful enough. However, Lord, please stay with me, because I just dare not go on alone. Thank you, Lord. Amen.

30. Doing something about it

Most written invitations have R.S.V.P. on the bottom, to ensure that a very accurate idea of the numbers of guests attending the function will be obtained. 'No' is also a reply, as is no reply at all, even if this is not recommended, if only from the point of view of common courtesy. Personally, I cannot think of Jesus without being deeply aware of this being God's invitation to become part of his family, by accepting the invitation to be one of his children. 'Unless you repent, and become like little children, you cannot enter the kingdom of heaven.' On one occasion Jesus said that, when he comes again, he really won't have to judge the world. The word he spoke will judge us. If he had not come and spoken the word, we would have an excuse for our sins. The invitation has been issued loud and clear, and our answer is either yes or no. Jesus said that we are either for him, or against him. There cannot be a middle road. Failure to accept the invitation and respond to it is considered as rejection.

The message of Jesus has been proclaimed all down through the ages. 'They who accept you, accept me, and they who reject you are rejecting the one who sent you.' We cannot serve two masters. Jesus is single-minded in his commitment to us, and he awaits some kind of similar generosity from us. Not, of course, that we are capable of anything like the same generosity as Jesus. Far from it. We can, however, be very generous in our openness and good-will, even if we fall short in the achieving. We will never get it right, and, thankfully, that's not what is taken into account. The reward is promised to those of good-will, to those who make the effort, to those who are willing to try. The good soil of the gospel is sometimes thirty, sometimes sixty, and only sometimes one hundred per cent. Even the thirty per cent is reckoned as good, because it produced something, and didn't lie fallow. If Jesus stood in front of you now, and spoke a word to you, he very well might go over and sit down on a chair, while he awaits to see what your response to that message is! His uttering of the message is but half the picture, and it awaits your response for completeness.

A new priest arrived in the parish. It was the first Sunday morning, and everyone was curious to know what he was like, and how good he was as a preacher. His sermon was very good, and made a good impression on all his hearers. There was a full house the following Sunday, because word had got out, and many others came along. There was general surprise when he preached exactly the same sermon as the previous Sunday. His listeners accepted this, believing it was because so many of today's congregation were not here last Sunday, and they needed to be brought up-to-date. The following Sunday, however, there was universal disquiet and grumbling, when the priest preached the very same sermon for the third Sunday! This became a matter of serious concern, when the same happened the fourth and the fifth Sunday! This was too much, and a delegation was selected to approach him, to sort out the impasse. Three little old ladies called to see the priest. They were slightly embarrassed, while being quietly confident that they had a responsibility to those who sent them.

They began 'That is a very good sermon you preached last Sunday, Father.' 'Oh, thank you very much,' replied the priest. 'It's really kind of you to call to tell me that.' 'Father, we were just wondering if you were aware of what has been happening these past few Sundays.' 'What is that?' asked the priest, in all innocence. 'What we mean to say, Father, is to ask you, if you don't mind, because we were told to ask you: Do you know any other sermon? Do you know that you have preached the same sermon for the last five Sundays?' 'Oh, of course, I know that', replied the priest. 'But, Father, if you don't mind us asking you, you do have other sermons, don't you?' 'Sure I have', said the priest. 'I have lots of other sermons.' 'But, Father, just for the sake of those who sent us, when could we expect you to move on to one of the other sermons?' 'I can assure you', said the priest, 'I'm looking forward to moving on to one of the other sermons, and I'll do so at the first possible opportunity. I promise you

most solemnly that I will willingly move on to the second sermon just as soon as I see you doing something about that first
one'!

The word of God is accompanied by the grace to respond, and to
carry out the word. It not only has an R.S.V.P., but it has a stamp-
addressed envelope, with the proper reply included! All I need do
is hear the message, decide that is what I want, accept the message,
and resolve to respond to that message. I am even supplied with the
grace to act on the message. That is why it makes no sense to continue
with sermon after sermon, if there is no response to any of them!
Jesus speaks of shaking the dust of such a place from our feet, and
getting out of town. I may be responsible for speaking the message,
but I certainly cannot take responsibility for whether others
respond to that or not. I am not God! The most I can do for another
is to heal sometimes, to help often, and to care always. If I think I
can always help or always heal, I become a nuisance. I speak the
message, and I stand back. The response may still come, even if the
delay appears to be indefinite. Just as I may invite another to a
response, so am I faced with my own need to respond to the Lord.
There can be quite a gap between the invitation and the response. I
certainly can clearly identify occasions when I decided to do something about an idea that had been around for a while. There is nothing more powerful than an idea whose time has come. Again and
again, I heard the message, and then, one day, almost completely
out of the blue, I made a decision to act on it. 'The road to hell is
paved with good intentions'. 'Not all who call me 'Lord' will enter
the kingdom of heaven', says Jesus. Calling him ' Lord', if he is not
Lord, will not get us very far.

Once again, I see here a reality that we can so easily over-look. Jesus
told us to 'watch and pray', in other words, to be awake, alert, on
our guard. The moment of grace comes by at the least expected
times, and, like Bartemaeus in the gospel, Jesus of Nazareth will
continue to 'pass by', unless I decide to stop him, and ask for the
miracle. This present moment will never ever be again. I remember
reading a poem some years ago about a man who was genuinely
trying to be a Christian. He was busy in his office, when a scruffy
long-haired youth walked in, chewing bubble-gum, with a guitar
on his back. He said he had just come by to say 'hello'. 'Hello' the

man replied, with undisguised sarcasm. The youth just stood there, saying nothing. The man had so much to do, he certainly had no time to waste on small talk with such an obvious layabout. After some embarrassing minutes of silence, the young man left. The last line of the poem was 'Problem with Jesus, he always seems to come at the wrong time'! One of the extraordinary things about Jesus, however, is that he seems to keep returning, giving us yet another chance. When he spoke to his apostles about forgiveness, he spoke of seventy times seven, which was a Hebrew way of describing something that goes on without limit. We could all be in serious trouble if the message or the invitation was issued once only! On the other hand, of course, I just cannot continue trusting that the message will be issued ad infinitum, without any response from me. I know there must surely come a time when my deafness is seen to be permanent …

Lord Jesus, I ask you, please keep at me, even if the response is slow in coming! I hope and pray that I do have the good-will, but I am also aware of a tendency to delay, put off, hold back. Please, Lord, continue to speak your word to me, and I trust that the Spirit within your word will never allow that word to remain barren. Lord, I have to trust you in this one, and I am truly thankful that I can. Don't give up on me, Lord! Amen.

31. Quality rather than quantity

The word of God is very different from any other word that can be spoken. If, for example, I tell you that Jesus Christ is Lord, and I write that on a blackboard, I must make a very clear distinction about what I have just done. To someone from China, the writing on the blackboard would look like some sort of prehistoric hiero-glyphics. However, for me, as a Christian, there is a truth contained in those words, and it is only God's Spirit who can reveal that. In other words, I can say it, and write it, but only God's Spirit can reveal it. From me you may get a fact, but from God's Spirit you get a truth. It is absolutely vital for the preacher and teacher of God's word to keep this basic fact in sight at all times. When a word is from God, it is shot through and through with power, it is inspired, it contains within it whatever it takes to be able to respond to, and to act on that word. Obviously then, the power of the preacher doesn't come from the number of words used! And, of course, the power of the preacher is a non-factor thing, because the power is in the word, and not in the speaker. I can, of course, ask the Spirit to anoint and empower my words, and I can certainly expect this to happen.

It is a wise person who practises what he preaches, and it is a fool who preaches what he practises! The word that I speak must pass through my own heart first. That way, I am the one most likely to be 'converted' by the words I speak. I remember reading a book one time by a famous Anglican preacher from the end of the last century, and the beginning of this one, and he gave quite a dramatic account of a personal conversion that took place during one of his own ser-mons! Suddenly, he heard what he was saying, he stopped, and broke down in tears. The congregation realised what was happen-ing, and they all burst out in songs of praise and thanks! (This is what encourages me to keep preaching!) Yes, indeed, the word I speak must first pass through my heart, because it is only when I speak from the heart that I speak to the heart. Preaching is never about talking heads! The people get enough of that on television. The oil prospectors have a rule: If you don't strike oil after a certain length of time, then stop boring! The same goes for the preacher! The preacher who doesn't know how to finish his sermon is like a nervous pilot. He is just about to touch down and land, when he takes off again for another circle! This can result in a crash-landing, when he runs out of juice! I would love to try out the following test on a preacher, as he leaves the sacristy to go out on the Altar: 'Tell me now, in one sentence, what you hope the people will know when you have finished your sermon.' I honestly believe that, if he cannot summarise his sermon in one sentence, he is not yet ready to give it.

It was a little village down in the south-west of Ireland. The parish priest was annoyed and frustrated by the local yokels who knelt on one knee on the cap at the back of the church, and nothing, but nothing could shift them nearer the altar. It is in the 'old days', and so he decided to have a Mission, and he'd bring in the Redemptorists, the commandos of those days, and they might succeed in putting some of the fear of God into that shower. Anyhow, the word got out, and it was a few days before the first week of the Mission, which was for the men. There was universal agreement among the men of the village to boycott the Mission, to have nothing to do with it.

The opening night of the Mission arrived, the missioner came out on the altar, complete with biretta, crucifix, turnip watch, and sheaves of paper, with his sermon notes. He looked down the church, and was completely taken aback to notice that there was one solitary man in the church. He lived out at the back of the mountain, he hadn't been in town all week, and he hadn't heard of the boycott. The priest came down towards the man, and said 'I'm supposed to preach a Mission here tonight, and you're the only one here. What do you think I should do? Should I go ahead, or just call the whole thing off?' The people in that part of Ireland have the reputation of not answering questions, or, at least, of answering one question with another question. 'Oh, Father, I wouldn't know, Father. I'm only a simple man, Father, and I live out at the back of the mountain. But I tell what, Father. I have twelve hens, and when I go out to feed them in the morning, if only one of them comes when I call, I feed her.' 'Oh, I see', says the priest, as he headed for the pulpit to feed the one solitary hen who had turned up!

He finished over an hour later, having covered everything from Adam and Eve till the Second Coming of the Lord! He then approached your man to get an opinion. 'Well, how was that? Are you happy enough with that?' Here, you will notice, is another question! 'Oh, Father I wouldn't know the answers to them sort of questions at all. I'm only a simple man, Father, and I live out at the back of the mountain. But I'll tell one thing, Father: I have twelve hens, and when I go to feed them in the morning, and only one comes when I call, I will, of course, feed her, but you can be sure, Father, that I won't give her the whole bucket'!

I remember an incident, from many years ago, when I was in my second year in a Teachers' Training College. In those days, we completed one year training, went out teaching for four years, and then returned for the second, and final year. One of our professors for the nuts and bolts of teaching practice ('Practical Pedagogy' might make a greater impression!) gave us a simple questionnaire to complete. We were to look at all the teachers we had in the Training College, mark down strengths and weaknesses (for very private circulation only!), give them a mark out of ten, and make specific recommendations as to how they could improve their approach, their personality, and their presentation. We weighed into this project with gusto, and with undeniable smugness. The task was now complete, and we were waiting to see what would now be done with this wealth of wisdom and wistful wit we had so graciously provided. We were given a blow to the solar plexus, however, when we were asked to now put pen to paper, and answer the very same questions as we imagined they might be answered by the pupils we had been teaching over the previous four years! I can only speak for myself, when I say that I needed that! I include that incident here, just in case any of my readers might have read thus far, and be sure of being able to identify someone else who fits the picture! We all know someone else who could benefit from every word of wisdom we hear! As Christians, the very same yardstick applies to all of us.

For example, I am writing a letter of sympathy to a friend, following a bereavement. I might easily fall into the trap of believing that the length and extent of what I have to say might be more helpful than the depth and sincerity of the words I might use. There are times when we have to make a phone call, write a letter, or visit a friend in trouble. We would be most unhelpful if we thought that they needed 'the whole bucket'! If I speak from the heart, I speak to the heart. When I go on and on, I probably have moved up into the head, and talking heads only compound the problem. Jesus said the Pharisees believed that, by multiplying prayers, they were more sure of getting God's attention! In fact, he said that we should never worry what we should say, when we speak as Christians, because the Spirit within would give us words that no one would be able to resist.

Lord, please help me take you, and your word seriously. One word from you, and I am healed. Please say that word, Lord. Help me apply the same principle in my prayers. I do want to be honest, sincere, and direct when I turn to you in prayer. To open out the canvas fully, and let you have total access. Spirit of God, please free me from any desire to impress God when I pray! Amen.

32. We are all sinners

I referred to a Teacher Training College in the previous reflection. Let us return there for a few moments. Some years ago I attended a fortieth class reunion. As we gathered, I thought we looked rather like a modern-day Dad's army! I certainly thought that all the others had aged a great deal over the years! I hadn't met most of them in the previous forty years, and it was a very moving occasion. I was the only priest present, and I was asked to lead in a Eucharistic celebration. As a gospel, I chose the story of the Pharisee and the Publican. In summary, I said 'Forty years ago, in this hallowed spot, we were given all the rules, regulations, and commandments. We learned all the proper definitions and prayers, and we were programmed for nothing less than perfection! Not only that, but we were being sent out to convert all the other less fortunates! This country would never be the same again! In effect, we were put in the Holy of Holies (with the Pharisee), and we were told to stay there, to keep all the rules, and we would get to heaven, and become very 'holy' in the process. (Keep the rule, and the rule will keep you, was what we were told). Now, forty years later, I just hope that we all have succeeded in seeing the craziness of such a stance, that we have long since got out of the Holy of Holies, and that, by now, we're well on our way to the back, where the publican is. If, before we die, we actually have reached that place where we can sincerely say 'Oh God, be merciful to me, a sinner', then, at last, we will have reached a level of wholeness and holiness, and will be ready for heaven.'

To become holy is to arrive at a conviction that I am a much bigger sinner than I ever thought I was! The closer I come to God, the more obvious the contrast. Being willing to name, claim, and tame my own demons, is a giant step towards truth, and that directly involves the Holy Spirit, the spirit of truth. To be touched by this Spirit of Truth relative to my own sinfulness leads to a life beyond my wildest dreams. It should end, for all time, the judgements, the condemnations, and the disdain that I might feel towards my fellow sinners. It would enable me look at someone who is responsible for some serious deviation, and say, with total conviction 'There go I, but for the grace of God.' I can claim no credit whatever for the parents I had, for the home in which I grew up, or my country of origin. I could have been any one of those people, of whatever colour, of whatever country, of whatever crime. The more I get in touch with who I am, and with what goes on within, the more my compassion, empathy, and understanding expands. Any compassion I have in life has not come from a text book, or from a series of lectures, or from a programme on compassion. It has come directly from my own personal experience of my own personal brokenness. The two main conditions for entering heaven is, firstly, to be a sinner, and, secondly, to openly admit and accept that fact. That applies equally to the heaven that is now, and the heaven that will be hereafter. The road to heaven is heaven, and God has nothing for me when I die that is not available to me now. I spoke earlier about a life beyond my wildest dreams. That is heaven, and it begins right now, as soon as I am willing and ready to accept and to live within the realities of who and what I am. If I went to live at the North Pole, I am still an Irishman. If I became a naturalised citizen of any country in the world, carrying that country's passport, I am still an Irishman! Even in heaven, I'll still be a sinner!

As a Catholic priest, I am telling this story about a minister of another Christian church, but, for the purpose of re-telling, I will leave all possible changes to the whim of the teller! This minister was down on his luck, his flock had dwindled, and interest in him and in his message was at an all-time low. One day, he decided to pack in the whole thing. He would look for some other kind of work, and, he reasoned, he would continue to do good wherever that would lead him. He was in for a great surprise, however, because all efforts to obtain alternative employment came to naught. In his desperation, he was compelled to take a job at the local zoo. Even there, the job promised him was not yet available, and, so, he was offered a temporary job to tide him over. The gorilla had died, and a replacement would take about two months. The children were very disappointed, and the visitors to the zoo had dropped noticeably. They were desperate, and in their quandary, they made a suggestion to the minister. He was asked if he would mind dressing up in a gorilla outfit! All he had to do, he was told, was to lie in the sun, to walk around occasionally, to eat a few bananas, and, perhaps to jump up and down a few times. For certain spells, he could even move in out of sight, and have a meal.

Beggars can't be choosers, so he decided to give it a go. Very soon, he discovered that it wasn't too bad, after all. When he rolled around, the children screamed with delight. Everyone was taking his photo, and whenever he showed any signs of life, the crowds quickly gathered. Very soon, he was thinking that he now was receiving much more attention that he did when he was in the pulpit!

This went on for several weeks, and the minister was identifying with the role more and more each day. One day he really felt in great form, full of pep, and not a little devilment! He jumped up, caught an over-head bar, and began to swing to and fro. The children were enraptured, as they cheered him on. This encouraged him no end, and, unfortunately, in no time at all, he got so involved in the act, that he got totally carried away. He began to swing faster and faster, and to rise higher and higher. At the height of one of the swings, his hands (paws?!) slipped, and he went flying in over a partition, and landed on his back in the cage next door. He was picking himself up, when, lo and behold, a huge tiger was approaching him. He panicked, forgot he was supposed to be a gorilla, and he began to holler 'Help! Help!' To which the tiger responded in a firm under-breath voice 'Shut up, you fool! I'm a minister too!'

It matters naught who we are, where we live, what we work at, each of us is a sinner. It is often so much easier for us to see the obvious in the other person. 'From what delusions it would free us, if we could see ourselves as others see us'! One of the clearest aspects of the gospel is the different levels of acceptance afforded Jesus. He came looking for sinners. Many sinners recognised him for what he was, and they flocked to him. The religious people were highly offended that Jesus, or anyone else, should suggest that they were sinners. In summary, they utterly despised those they considered sinners, and they reserved equal scorn for those who had anything to do with such sinners.

A very central part of the role of the Spirit is to convict us of sin. The Spirit leads into all truth, and one of the basic truths is that we are sinners. A deep personal conviction about sin and sinfulness in my life is a pre-requisite for fully accepting Jesus, who firstly, is Saviour, and who then becomes Lord. Because I am a sinner, my fist encounter with Jesus is always as Saviour. In a moment of grace, some fore-shadowing and fore-echoing of that final cry of the holy person begins to form on my lips, and in my heart 'Oh God, be merciful to me, a sinner.' From that moment, I am on my way to wholeness, to holiness, and to heaven.

Spirit and Breath of God, you are a Spirit of truth, and if I am ever to walk in the ways of truth, then I'm depending on you to lead me there. Jesus said that part of the truth would be to convict us of sin. Please continue to open my eyes to the need for salvation, repentance, and redemption in my life. Thank you. Amen.

33. The choice is ours

Again and again, in these reflections, I have stated that God offers everything, and he then stands back. His respect for my free-will, and the free decisions that I myself must make, means that God is super-sensitive to my right to say yes or no. The gospels tell us that Jesus came for the rise and for the fall of many. Not for the automatic rise of anyone. The outcome depends completely on my co-operation, or refusal to co-operate. Jesus offers me peace, but I'm totally free to live in misery and die of ulcers, if I want to! We all come across those times in our lives where we find ourselves at a crossroads. We have to make a decision, to opt for one choice or the other. 'I came to an intersection in the road, I took the road less travelled, and that made all the difference.' Jesus says that he is the Way, not one of the ways. I can travel any way I choose, but it is only in his way that his promises can be expected to hold up. It is only when I travel in his way that I can expect his Spirit to guide me.

Without wishing to be too mystical or theologically technical, there are constant moments of grace in our lives. This is represented in the gospels by the phrase 'Jesus of Nazareth is passing by.' The blind man, the little woman in the crowd, the lepers, etc., they all had a choice. They could let Jesus pass by, or they could stop him, ask him, and be healed. Jesus didn't go around healing anybody. He went around with the power to heal, and the person on the roadside had to make a decision. There were many people in Jesus' time who died of leprosy, for example, even though Jesus passed close to where they were. Once again, the law could have come in the way. Lepers had to keep at a distance from others, and their strict adherence to this edict may have superseded their desire to be healed, and so nothing happened. There were others, however, and they very definitely wanted to be healed, and they knew that Jesus could heal them. Nothing, but nothing would get in their way, and they ended up healed. There is no way they would miss out on the moment of grace. They grabbed it with both hands, because of an inner hunger. 'He fills the hungry with good things,' Mary says.

I need to elaborate on what I see as a moment of grace. This requires some reflection, because it may not be easy to put this in words, or to understand the full meaning behind the words that are used. This is what I think: This present moment is a moment of grace, if I am ready and willing to be open to it. In other words, every moment has the potential to be a moment of grace. Every moment is graced, but I may not avail of it. It is difficult for us to comprehend that, because we might tend to imagine that I would need to be in touch with God at all times, that I would need to be fully alert for every passing moment, that I would have to be praying and muttering yes with every breath I take! A sure recipe for breakdown! It is not any of the above. Basically, it is a question of attitude. If the attitude is right, where God is allowed run the show, and I am on standby, awaiting his word, then there is always something happening. Alot of the time I will not be conscious of anything happening, but like the baby getting teeth and hair, there is on-going growth. Some of the times I will be very conscious of what is happening, I will be aware of the call, and will be allowed to have a personal input into this. All of this is in God's hands, and I have no need to worry, because that is a much safer situation than if everything was in my hands! When particular moments of grace come along, I will know, and, through the action of God's Spirit within, I will be ready to avail of them. It is the role of the Spirit to remind us, because, quite often, we just forget, or lose sight of the vision.

This is a true story that I personally witnessed. I was growing up in the country. We did not have electricity, and we were used to tilley lamps, oil lamps, hurricane lamps, wet and dry batteries for wirelesses (before they became radios!), etc. All of my family, at one time or another, had visited cousins up in the big city, and so we were aware of electricity, and the marvellous benefits that went with such an amenity. I remember well the great excitement engendered by the news that 'they' (?) were coming to put electricity in everybody's house over the next year. We were all agog. Electric kettles, ovens, lights in outhouses and farmyard, and a wireless that didn't die in the middle of an interesting pro-gramme. To us, there was no end to the possibilities.

Some time later, the excitement mounted when word arrived that men were seen leaving poles lying on the side of the road, at fixed distances, and, very soon, those poles were hoisted and erected. This first stage was in near the local town. The postman kept us informed on progress each day, and, whenever any of us had reason to go into town, we were sure to check out what was happening, and to report back all the details.

Finally, the great day arrived! The poles were just outside our house, the men were running wires in all directions, and, even-tually, the big switch-on took place. That was a day to remember for a country kid! It was about one week later when I made a startling discovery. Over the road from me lived an elderly brother and sister, and they didn't take the electricity! They were, of course, free not to take it, but, at the time, I didn't know or understand that. I stood outside their house, and I looked at the wires that passed some yards from their front door. I even peeped in the window to assure myself that their oil lamp was still in use. I asked my mother the reason for all this. She explained about choices, decisions, personal freedom, etc., but I wasn't very convinced, and my reactions of then are just as vivid today, as I write this. I was told they got electricity some years later, but, by then, I had moved on.

When I began to get to grips with life, and with what life involves, I saw this earlier situation in a different light (no pun intended!) Especially when I came to reflect on the God-dimension of our lives. Jesus of Nazareth is passing by, just like the Electricity Supply Board! Nobody has to avail of it. I can opt to remain in darkness, if I so choose. Jesus is never going to gate-crash anybody's party. He will enter by invitation only. He came as a light to the world, to a world in darkness, and in the shadow of death. He invites us to fol-low him so that we walk not in darkness. Notice, however, that it is invitation all the way. I'm sure we all have come across situations where it seemed impossible to drag individuals or institutions into the twentieth century. With Jesus, there is no dragging. It is interest-ing to note that, with this couple, when they did decide to avail of the electricity, it was still there for them. God's graces are always on offer, always available. I think we would all be in trouble if they had to be accepted at the very first offer! To continue the analogy of the electricity, I think of God's grace in terms of something, which, the more I accept, the more becomes available. In other words, accepting the electricity is but the beginning of a process. If I were to monitor the progress in one of those houses over the past fifty-five years, it would be very interesting. It's been a long long journey from that first bulb to the present computer, microwave, etc. They continue to build on that initial acceptance, and none of us knows what exactly the future may hold for homes that have the basics of electric power.

Lord Jesus, you came as the Light of the world. It scares me to think that I can refuse that light, and continue to live in darkness. Please, Lord, flood my heart and my whole life with your light. Let me bring your light to those in darkness. I offer myself as a messenger, Lord. Please use me, send me, empower me, enlighten me. Amen.

34. God's ways are not our ways

Frank Sinatra had a memorable hit with a song called 'I did it my way'. Bing Crosby is remembered for a movie called 'Going my way'. Somewhere in the middle of it all I think of us humans starring in our own show, which we could call 'I still insist on doing things my way'! Jesus said that he was the Way, and nobody could come to the Father in any other way. I am, of course, free to travel in any way I choose, but those other ways do not lead to life, in the short or long term. How often have we heard it said that 'God's ways are not our ways'. The generations before us seemed to have a very firm grip on that concept, and there seemed to be a great desire to remain open to whatever God wanted, whatever road he called us to travel.

It's really easy for us to live in our heads. We can reason things out, rationalise our decisions, and intellectualise our motives. The world in which we live out our existence presents this phenomenon on a daily basis. We see it in politics, in the media, in business. It is the sensible way to act, the common sense thing to do. It can be promoted, defended, justified. It is logical, obvious, and reasonable. All of that is important to someone who lives in the head. To such people, it must be most uncomfortable to hear Scripture speak of becoming a fool for the sake of the gospel, for the sake of Christ. This head-approach becomes a security anchor, and it can be scary to be asked to let go. It's only a fool who argues with a head-person, especially about some things like God and spirituality.

God and spirituality are essentially of the heart, and they will never make much sense up in the head. 'The children of this world' will always have a serious problem with the gospel of Jesus Christ, and, indeed, with Jesus Christ himself. Forgiving our enemies, turning the other cheek, giving away what is mine, all of that must seem absolute nonsense to someone with a world mind-set. St Paul says that the cross is a scandal to one group, and foolishness to another. God's Spirit lives in our hearts, and for those people who live in the heart, all of God's mysteries become realities. 'To you is given to understand the mysteries of the kingdom, but to the rest in parables,' Jesus told his apostles. This is revelation, and has very little to do with academic knowledge. Revelation literally means to 'lift the veil that covers something'. In other words, it's just barely covered, but, unless the veil is lifted, I'll never notice it. Revelation is what God does. For the person who lives in the heart, life is continuous revelation. God is continually revealing the mysteries, I am constantly aware of his on-going presence and activity. God, the creator, is always creating. 'I make all things new.'

I know it's obvious, but it needs to be repeated again and again: I don't understand God, or the workings of God. There are times, indeed, and I just cannot understand why God does things this way, and not the other way. I am glad, however, that God is God, because he knows what he's doing, and I shudder to think what might happen if I were allowed run the show for a while! We have all come across those people who are described as 'not belonging to this world'. They are dreamers, visionaries, people who see something the rest of us seem to miss. Indeed, we may sometimes rejoice that we're not like them, because it is difficult to make sense out of what they do, and, it can be important to us to make sense out of things. I speak of missionaries, workers in the Third World, those people who are always seen to be charging the windmills, to be endeavouring to hold back the tide with a spoon, to hold a finger in the dike. How on earth can they keep going?

Supposing God had given us the job of arranging for his coming into the world, how do you think we'd go about working out the details? I've no doubt we'd begin by forming a committee, and electing a chairperson. Then the chairperson would appoint various sub-committees, each of which would attend to one particular aspect of the project. If we ran true to form, there would be a welcoming committee, a banquet committee, an entertainment committee, a publicity committee, a security committee, and, God forgive us, there'd even be a finance committee. The chairperson might decide on a public relations committee, in charge of 'no hurt feelings', whose first order of business would be to make a survey. In the chairperson's words 'Let us give everybody an opportunity to be heard. For something like this, too much hassling wouldn't look good.' A questionnaire is printed, setting forth a number of key questions, beginning with 'How shall we bring God into the world – in a spaceship, in an open limousine leading a motorcade of world dignitaries, in solemn religious procession at one of the world's great shrines?'

But what about the possibility of God coming in an obscure dingy stable? Certainly no one on the committee would have thought of that!

Yes, indeed, God's ways are certainly not our ways, and nowhere is this more evident than in the way Jesus chose to walk among us. 'Nazareth? Can anything good come out of Nazareth?' was Nathaniel's question, when told where Jesus came from. I can think of many simple incidents in the gospel that used to puzzle me, back along the way. For example, when Jesus healed a man, he warned him not to tell anybody. That seemed strange, because if people were to follow him, then the more that knew of such miracles the better. That was my reasoning. I now believe that what Jesus was saying was: 'Don't tell others, because I certainly don't want anyone believing in me because of what I did for you. If they themselves are open to me, and allow me enter their lives, their faith will then be based on experience. They will have come and seen for themselves, and will not believe just because of something someone else told them.' Remember the shepherds at Bethlehem? 'Let us go to Bethlehem to see for ourselves this thing which the Lord has made known to us.' There's no mention of forming a committee! If I were to die this moment, it is possible that Jesus could ask me: 'Did you really come to believe that my Father loved you? I mean, did you come to believe that from your own personal experience, or did you believe it because somebody else told you?' A person could spend a full life-time on a First Communion level of spirituality. God is a very personal God. Jesus asked the apostles 'Who do people say that I am?', and, before they completed their answer, he added a further question 'And you, who do you say that I am?' I can never presume that Jesus is somewhere in the community, in the parish. If I do not experience him, hear him, see evidence of him, then, for me, he is not there. Even Mary and Joseph made that mistake one time. They were returning from Jerusalem, and they presumed Jesus was somewhere in the crowd. They discovered, however, that he was not there, and it was three days later before they found him. They found him, because they were looking for him, not just because they were looking for something, and they found Jesus. Christianity is about a person. It is not about some nice idea, or some high level of moral behaviour.

Lord Jesus, please help me become a person of the heart. Please keep me out of my head. I don't need committees, I don't need programmes. I love you, Lord, I welcome you, and I sure am glad you came. I have no idea, Lord, what would have happened to me if you hadn't come. It makes a whole eternal difference. Thank you, Lord, for coming the way you did. Amen.

35. Whose problem is it?

There is a new phenomenon now called co-dependency. There is someone with a problem, for example, an alcoholic. There is someone else, a spouse or a family member who gets 'sucked' into this person's problem. This second person has a need to protect the alcoholic from the evil consequences of his ways. This person covers up, tells lies, picks up the slack, – all with the very best of intentions, and with great love, even if misguided. Such a person is called a co-dependent. Another name is an enabler. In other words, without meaning it, such a person allows the alcoholic to go on drinking, while the debris is being cleared up behind. An alcoholic doesn't feel any need to stop drinking as long as there is an 'enabler' around! (We all need one!) With the very best of intentions, I can easily be contributing to the problem of the one I am trying to help. With misguided love, I can feed another person's weaknesses.

There is a personality profile known as The Enneagram, which is a system that divides personalities into nine separate sections. It dates back for many thousands of years, and, in my limited experience, it seems to be extraordinarily accurate. I belong to one of nine groups, with some of me in the group next to mine. For example, if I belong to group Two, I am a Helper. In general, I can be described as someone who helps others, but also someone who, for my very reason for existing, needs to help others. If I am a Two, then it is accepted that most of me belongs to this category, while having what is called 'a wing' in one of the nearest numbers. Part of me may belong to number One, the Perfectionist, because I like to have things the way they ought to be. Or part of me may belong to number Three, the Achiever, where I want to accomplish something, and have something to show at the end of the day. This reflection has little to do with the Enneagram! I refer to it just to show that I could be a number Two, someone with a compulsion to help others.

In this group, as with every other group, there is a healthy Two, an average Two, and an unhealthy Two. The unhealthy Two will rush with a tissue if you sneeze, and if you do not allow such ministration, this person is deeply hurt, because you do not appreciate all that is being done for you! In other words, such a person is meeting a personal need to be helpful. We all know people who are so anxious to help that they tend to take over a situation. And then, of course, there are others who are only too happy to let them do that! It can be difficult to live with boundaries, especially if the discipline in early life was inconsistent, or even non-existent. It is a good idea, sometimes, to ask myself, in a given situation, 'Whose needs am I meeting here?' I'm not suggesting that I don't have to meet my own needs. We all have needs, and we all have a need to be needed. No one person is an island; we are all part of the mainland of humanity, and we all need each other. The more I get my own act together, the more I am a source of blessing for all those around me. To live positively is to take responsibility for my place in the scheme of things, and to be open to become part of the solution, rather than settle for being part of the problem.

> A young father was pushing a buggy through a public park. His only son and heir was in the buggy, and the little guy was crying at the top of his voice. The father quickened his pace towards home, realising that he had remained outdoors longer than he had intended, and the screams were hunger pains. As he walked along, he spoke quietly and firmly. 'O.K., Donald, O.K. Donald. You're doing alright, Donald. Calm down now. Don't panic.'
>
> Meanwhile, there was a little old lady sitting on a park bench nearby, and she was genuinely impressed by how the father kept talking to the baby as he walked along. She got up, approached the buggy, looked in, and said 'Well now, Donald pet, what seems to be the matter? What's upsetting poor little Donald?' The father looked at her sheepishly, and said 'Actually, the baby's name is Stephen. I'm Donald'!

Not much of a story, perhaps, but it gives some food for thought! 'Let there be peace on earth, and let it begin with me.' The turmoil within my heart always comes out through my words and actions. The greatest contribution I can make towards peace in the world, is to ensure that I have peace within my own heart. Probably the most vulnerable human being on this earth is the baby in the womb. Every vibe and emotion of the mother is being transmitted, and the formation is already well under way. If the mother is unhappy with this pregnancy, and she does not want to have this baby, that inner sense of being rejected and unwanted is being imprinted on the baby's psyche for all time. The safest, most nurturing place for a new-born baby is in the arms of a mother who is at peace. This is a safe place, and blessed is the baby who finds it.

When Jesus speaks of peace, he offers us his peace, 'not the peace the world gives, which is fragile.' The first stage of life is the womb-life. It is there that my human nature is evolving, that my personality is being put together, that I am being 'knit together', to use a phrase from the Psalms. The second stage of life could be called the womb of life. As a Christian, I sometimes think of this as the womb of God, where I am being formed in the image of Jesus Christ. This can be as safe a place as I permit it to be. 'I will never forget you, my people ... Could a mother forget her baby, or a woman the child within her womb? Yet even if these forget, I will never forget my own.' The man in our story was desperately trying to ensure that he wasn't going to contribute any further stress to the child, by getting stressed himself. Inner emotions are transmitted through some sort of osmosis. God is love, and to nestle in that love is to be nurtured into security, to wholeness, to holiness. Surely there is a whole prayer-experience available to those who take time out to reflect on being totally surrounded with God's love, something like the very air around me. To sit, and let that thought float around, and, hope-fully, settle down in the heart. To experience some sort of immunity there from all the evils and all the dangers. 'If God is for us, who can be against us?' To think of God in terms of the total atmosphere can help to make my God a little bigger! The bigger my God, the smaller my problems! Sometimes my God is so small that my problems weigh me down.

There is an old Chinese proverb which says 'If each before his own door swept, the whole village would be clean.' Looking around the world today, it is always a sign of hope when some one person somewhere turns to God, and offers that one human heart as an embassy for his Spirit and his peace. Each of us is God's touch-person in the lives of others. I cannot give what I haven't got. On the other hand, if I open my heart, God will fill it. Such a person needs only to be in a place to bring peace to that place. The words channel and instrument are frequently used to describe our role as Christians. I am convinced that if I went up the mountains to live in a cave, if I have God's peace and power within, there will be a path up the side of the mountain in a few years, as others gather to receive what I have.

Spirit and Breath of God, source of wisdom, the one who enables us notice the obvious. Please continue to lead me into the mysteries of the kingdom, and into the enlightened common sense of wholesomeness. Let there be peace, and let it begin with me. I offer my heart as a base, as a spring-board for you to touch the hearts of those around me. Thank you, Lord, for wanting to include me in this. Amen.

36. Jesus at the door

Jesus didn't come to be locked in a tabernacle! In fact, he didn't come on earth to be locked up anywhere! Maybe the need is on our part, to keep him under some sort of control! On the morning of the Ascension, the apostles stood looking up into heaven, where Jesus was seen to go beyond their sight. Suddenly two angels appeared on either side of them, and asked 'Why do you stand here looking up to heaven? The Jesus whom you have seen go, will return again, just as you have seen him go.' When Jesus returns in glory at the end of time, his plan will be completed. The other two kingdoms will have run their course, will have had their day. The kingdom of this world will have come to an end, and the kingdom of Satan will be confined to its own horror for all eternity, no longer able to hurt or lie to any of God's children. At last, the kingdom of God will be firmly established, and the harvesting will be complete.

Let me reflect briefly on what I think about the coming of Jesus Christ. When Jesus came that first Christmas night, this was to set the snowball in motion, as it were. When he comes at the end of the world, that will be to complete the work set in motion on that first occasion. In between those two comings, Jesus comes to us every day, and every moment of every day, if I am open to such visitations. I think it is important that we understand what is entailed in these daily comings of Jesus. He comes to us in our brokenness, in our sinfulness, just exactly as we are. If, like Peter, I recoil, and don't allow him wash my feet through a ministry of total acceptance, then, of course, 'you cannot belong to my kingdom.' Only those people who allow Jesus come to them, without denial, pretence, without trying to be anything they're not, only those people are being prepared for the harvest of that second coming. This can be so difficult for religious people to understand, because it seems so simple and so easy that there just has to be a 'catch' in it somewhere! While I still retain the need to earn my salvation, then, of course, I just cannot avail of the offer. Jesus will not be permitted come to me day after day. It's not so long ago since the idea of receiving Communion more than once a year was unheard of. When I was a child, we went to Confession on Saturday if we wished to receive Communion on Sunday. We were forever scrubbing and polishing our souls, meriting indulgences and earning graces, all with the purpose that when Jesus came to us in Communion, he would have nothing to do, because we had taken care of everything! There is a cosmetic, antiseptic dimension to religion, as if we were holding God out on forceps, or, worse still, we think of him holding us at arm's length. Nothing could be farther from the truth. Those everyday comings of Jesus are made available because he knows just how vulnerable we are, how lonely we can be, how lost we can feel. 'I did not come to condemn the world ... Neither do I condemn you.' At the beginning of creation, God began with a time of great love, where he walked with his people in the Garden of Plenty. When that was rejected, he commenced a time of great mercy, when, in Jesus, he would walk with us in our brokenness, cry with us, suffer with us, stay with us. The third and final time will be one of infinite justice, when everything unclaimed, everything hidden, everything denied, will be hung out in public, and all will be exposed to the light of his truth, and the judgement of his justice. During this present stage, I can always expect Jesus to come to me, and I can always open my heart to receive and welcome him. It is for me that he comes. If I had it together, he would have no need to come, and the more convinced I am of my need for him, the more free he is to effect his redemption and salvation in me.

The old monk was at prayer in the chapel. It was a quiet moment, and he cherished these moments greatly. He felt a deep sense of the Lord's presence, and a profound sense of gratitude and privilege. Suddenly, he was fully alert and wide-eyed, as Jesus stood there in front of him in full physical form. Jesus smiled, and looked at him, and the monk's spirit was melting with the sheer rapture and joy of it all.

Suddenly, the door bell rang. It was that time of day when the down-and-outs came by for a cup of tea, and a sandwich. What was he to do? Without saying anything, he got up, left the chapel, and went off to attend to whoever was at the door. It was at least ten minutes later when he returned. He was beside himself with delight, because the vision was still there as he left it. He fell on his knees, and thanked Jesus for awaiting his return. Jesus smiled once again. 'If you had not gone to take care of that poor man at the door, I would not have stayed. That also was me you cared for, and so I stayed to say "thank you".'

Going back to the two men in white speaking to the apostles on the morning of the Ascension, we could easily paraphrase their words thus: 'Men of Galilee, why do you stand here looking up into heaven? The Jesus you have seen leaving is now to be found all around you. He is to be found in the outcasts, the marginalised, the down-trodden, the tramp at the front door. He takes whatever you do to the least of those as having been done for him personally.' Once again, I see great material for reflection here. Just imagine, if you can, what it would really be like if you actually believed, and acted on the belief, that whatever you do for others, Jesus takes as being done for him? I know that the theory and the idea is generally known and accepted, but I speak here of some inner conviction, a situation where the coin drops, the lights come on, and I know, I believe, I act. What a witness that would be! What a change that would make in the world if that spark blew into a flame and ignited the hearts of others! 'I have come to cast fire upon the earth, and how can I be at rest until it is enkindled?'

From time to time the Lord sends someone among us to live out that truth, and to inspire others to do likewise. Usually they have founded Congregations to care for people who were being neglected. One thinks of Edmund Rice (Christian Brothers), Catherine McAuley (Mercy), Nano Nagle (Presentation), Mary Aikenhead (Charity). These were people who came to know that truth, to believe it, and to act on it. These people effected change in the lives of thousands, because they dared take Jesus at his word, and act on that word. This is the role of the prophet, to interpret the present, and to call others to join them in rescuing the present. They are the leaven Jesus speaks of, the salt that preserves, the light that dispels the darkness.

It is a very special grace, indeed, to get the balance right between the Jesus in the chapel, and the Jesus at the front door! The Jesus at the front door is usually more demanding, and less attractive, and, therefore, it can easily be tempting to stay in the chapel, put down my head and keep praying! How often I have come across people who object to the sign of peace at Mass! Such an unnecessary distraction from the intensity of their prayers! When I suggested earlier that there was great scope for reflection here, I was thinking that this truth is something that only God's Spirit could reveal to me, or continue to remind me of its reality.

Lord Jesus, I know that you are anywhere I choose to find you. Please help me find you in my own brokenness, and at those times when I feel most alone. I ask that your Spirit enable me to be deeply sensitive to your presence in those around me. I ask for the faith to accept this fact, for the times when your presence is not so obvious. Amen.

37. Me or us?

I wrote a book one time called *The Higher Power*. The title was unfortunate, perhaps, because, unknown to me at the time, this was the accepted title for God as understood by people in Twelve-Step Recovery programmes. I know some people who bought the book, believing it to be part of A.A. literature. Fortunately, however, they found the book useful, because, in essence, it spoke of the same situations, perhaps from slightly different angles. Anyhow, I began that book by speaking of my mother making bread. With thirteen kids to feed, she needed plenty of flour, and, thankfully, plenty of raisins. I suggested that if I took the dough, ready for the oven, and looked at that as representing human nature, it might help our understanding. The raisins represent human weaknesses, and the dough, as human nature, could well have a health-warning on it! There are elements within that are not conducive to human well-being. I then spoke of my mother rolling out that dough, and with a glass tumbler turned upside down, and dipped regularly in dry flour, she proceeded to cut out small scones. Each scone has a different combination of the raisins, and each scone represents each one of us human beings. Each of us is a scone from that dough. We are all part of a great whole, and no one is an island. Very selfish people either don't know, or don't care that their behaviour impinges on the lives of others. There is a communal dimension to sin. I go into a large supermarket in town. I just want to buy a few items, pay for them, and leave. However, I have a feeling of being watched on a television screen up in some room, that man standing over there is a store detective, and he notices me, and I'll probably have to pay a few extra pence at the check-out, – all because people come into this store to steal. Now I have never stolen anything from this store, but I am being directly adversely effected by the behaviour of others. Similarly, there are areas of the city that have no public transport service after a certain hour at night. Most of the people having to walk home, or make other arrangements, are decent law-abiding citizens. A few people, from their area, however, did cause serious problems on late-night buses, and now everybody is suffering.

It has been well said that all that is needed for evil people to succeed is that good people should do nothing. Thank God for the doers, for those people who are aware of our collective responsibility. It is so easy to have tunnel vision, to see directly ahead, what is in my path only. This is a self-imposed form of solitary confinement, and it carries its own burden of loneliness. There are times when one could reasonably despair of there ever being peace and justice on this earth. Sometimes the tidal waves of selfishness and viciousness take on Satanic proportions. In more than one country lately, there has been evidence of genocide. This must surely be an abomination in the sight of God. This earth belongs to all of us, and the most handicapped child is on this earth with as much right as the greatest genius that ever lived. Part of my own reaction, when I think of these atrocities and injustices, is to get angry, and then I say 'Ah, here we go again!' My anger is only going to add to the accumulative anger out there. What is needed is love. It is difficult, however, to see how my love could actually effect a situation in Rwanda or in Bosnia. In my frustration, at times, I continue to reflect on the thought 'Supposing I stay at home, and start at home?' I don't know exactly what good this would do, but I have to believe it would be doing something. That so many people should die is a tragedy. That their deaths should be wasted, and go unnoticed is a disgrace. Even if I try to build a bridge towards some human being, because of my pain at what I read in the papers, that, at least, is something.

A young man knocked at the door of a house. 'Who is it?' asked a voice from within the house. 'It is me', said the young man. 'I have come to ask permission to marry your daughter.' 'You're not ready', said the voice from within. 'Go away, and come back next year.'

A year went by. The young man came back and knocked on the door again. 'Who is it?' asked the voice from inside. 'It's us', said the young man. 'We've come to ask your permission to marry.' The voice from within said 'Now you're ready to get married. Come on in.'

It takes two to make a marriage work! Marriage is a journey from falling in love into growing into love, a journey from looking at each other to looking forward in the same direction. There are generally four stages on this journey. The first stage is the honeymoon stage. My needs are being met by the other, which, in a subtle kind of way, is selfishness. It is often called infatuation, which comes from the Latin *ignus fatuous*, meaning a 'false fire'! It is based on feelings, and feelings, as we all know, do not last. Pity the couple who get married because they feel love for each other! Love is a decision. I cannot control feelings, whereas I can control decisions. Hopefully, of course, on the day of the wedding, the decision is accompanied by feelings of love. I can make that decision each and every day, and, hopefully, I will come to live today on today's decisions, not on a decision I made several years ago. The psychologists describe this stage as passive dependence, and the cartoonist would illustrate it with two people leaning on each other, and, if one walked away, the other would fall. The second stage is disillusionment. One morning, I waken up, and wonder what I got myself into! I realise now that you are not perfect after all! I begin to see you as you really are, and I'm not sure I actually like what I see! This is where the quitters quit, if they had not been warned that this stage was bound to come, as sure as day follows night. Hopefully, I also realise that you must now see me as I really am, and you, too, may not be over the moon about what you see! If we can bridge this gap, and begin to accept and love each other just exactly as we are, then, for the first time, we have begun to love each other. And this is what is called the third stage. The fourth stage is where something extraordinary has begun to happen. They are now in the twilight of their lives. A son calls to take them for a drive. He asks his dad where he would like to go, and he is asked 'What did your mother say? Did you ask her?' He goes into the garden to ask her, and he hears the exact same question 'What did daddy say? Did you ask him?' Each began the journey by having personal needs met, and each is now concerned only with what the other wants to do. They have arrived at loving each other!

I remember being at a funeral many years ago, of the father of a priest friend of mine. His parents were the proverbial Darby and Joan. I was wondering how Joe was going to manage his few words at his dad's funeral, because I knew that father and son had also grown close over the years. We all sat back, waiting what was going to be said. He caught us all by surprise with a one-sentence homily! He looked over at the coffin for a few seconds, and then he said 'My father was married to my mother for the past fifty-seven years, and he really did come to love her in that time.' They had set out together to do just that all those years ago, and they had succeeded. One of the greatest journeys possible to any human being. They had found love, they had found God. The nearest I'll ever come to seeing God on this earth, is if I ever come across two people who really love each other.

Holy Spirit and Breath of God, I ask you, please, to impress on my heart a firm conviction that I am not an island, but just part of a larger body. Please help me accept responsibility for the words and actions of mine that affect the lives of those around me. Create a sense of reverence in me for the beauty and the awesomeness of the over-all plan. Thank you, Lord, for including me as part of your plan. Amen.

38. How I see myself

I heard a story about a teacher in a country national school. The school inspector had called, and the teacher was whispering to him about a pupil in the front row. What he didn't know was that the pupil heard every word. The teacher was telling the inspector just how backward and stupid this pupil was. The inspector decided to test this for himself. He asked the simplest questions, and he got the wrong answers. Even the teacher was amazed, because he didn't think the lad was that stupid! After the inspector left, the teacher spoke to the lad. 'Surely, you knew the answers to some of those questions?' 'Oh, I did, sir, I did. But I heard you telling him how stupid I was, and I didn't want to let you down.' Formation begins very early in life. If a child is told often enough that he is stupid, he himself will come to accept and believe that after a while. The greatest good I can give to others is not to share my riches with them, but to reveal their riches to themselves. Pentecost is about God's Spirit coming to live in our hearts. When that happens, we are able to confirm others. Hence our sacrament of Confirmation. The person who hates herself hasn't one good word to say about someone else.

When God created anything, including people, 'He saw that it was good'. Herb Barks says 'God don't make no junk.' I have met people who believed they were an exception to that! Formation begins very early in life. There is an Irish idiom which says 'Praise the young, and they will come with you.' There is a wall-chart which speaks of how a child will develop by living with fear, criticism, scorn. This will have a direct influence on the adult later in life. The problem with children is we only get one shot at the formation process. It has been said 'Give me a child until he's four, and you can do anything you want with him after that.' All of this is like the hen and the egg scenario. If I don't have God's Spirit within, I cannot confirm others. I cannot give what I haven't got. ('Nemo dat quod non habet', as the Latins would put it). Children thrive on approval, as, of course, we all do. In children it is more evident. In many ways, the child and the adult are not so different. (Is it possible that the only real difference between a man and a boy, is that the man's toys are more expensive?!) I must confess that I don't like cats! (Sorry about that!) Anyhow, I am familiar with the purring of the cat in a situation where attention, approval, and love is forthcoming. We mightn't hear any sound, but I believe that humans purr also! There is a hunger for approval in all of us.

It frightens me to think that some people become what others programmed them to be. I have seen very ambitious parents, endeavouring to succeed through their children. They themselves didn't make it to college, so the next best thing is to ensure that their children do. This can, of course, be excellent, unless it is meeting a need in the parents to be able to speak to their friends a whole new language about life in Third Level education. Education comes from the Latin educare, meaning to lead out. It involves discovering and bringing out all the gifts and talents that are within. No point in sending Junior for piano lessons if there is no gift for music within. It is not possible to put in a gift (Inducation?). Nobody ever becomes fully educated. Most people live and die, and discover only about one quarter of the gifts within. That seems a woeful waste. The Power of Positive Thinking was an attempt to motivate people to go 'for it', to give it everything you have. Life is not unlike a computer. Feed in junk, and you'll get out junk!

> One day John made a strange find. He came upon an eagle's egg, and he decided to put it into the nest of a farmyard hen. In time the eaglet hatched with the hen's brood of chicks, and grew up with them. All his life the eagle did what the farmyard chicks did, thinking he was a chicken. He scratched in the yard for worms, insects, and scraps of food. He clucked, cackled, and he would thrash his wings and fly a few feet in the air.

> Years passed, and the eagle grew old. One day he saw a magnificent bird far above him, in the clear blue sky. He watched it glide majestically among the powerful wind currents, with scarcely a beat of its golden wings. The old eagle looked up in awe. 'Who's that?' he asked. 'That's an eagle, the king of the birds',

replied his neighbour. 'He belongs to the sky. We belong to the earth, we're chickens.' Eventually, the old eagle died a chicken. He had lived as a chicken, and he died a chicken, because that was what he thought he was.

I remember giving a one-day Retreat to a class of girls preparing for Confirmation. Having spent most of my life in schools, this was something I felt very at ease with, and I knew we had all enjoyed the day. Some days later, I met the mother of the one of the girls. She told me her daughter came home on cloud-nine! It was the best Retreat she had ever been on! I was one of the nicest persons she had ever met! The mother broke into her enthusiasm to ask her to recount something I had said, and the reply was 'He told me I had beautiful eyes'! (And I'm not sure if she remembered anything else!) I smiled when I heard this, because it is so typical of kids. I remember a lad I had in school one time who was proving to be a good swimmer. I kept encouraging him, and I convinced him that he was certainly above average. The confidence gained here spread over into his academic studies, and he began to work at that with the same belief that, here too, he was above average. What responsibility parents and teachers have when it comes to children! 'The child is father to the man'. The child being formed now is determining what the man will be later on.

When I was teaching in primary schools many years ago, there is something I used do after receiving a new class at the beginning of the school year. Usually these pupils had been together in other classes over the previous four or five years. I didn't know them, and I always felt it necessary to learn as much as I could about them. I would suggest a little experiment. I suggested that we were given a project, that required a great deal of research, many hours in the library, and much writing. I ask each pupil to write down the names of three other pupils in this class that she/he would pick to help with that project. I then collected the pieces of paper, and put them in my briefcase. Some days later, I had another suggestion. This time we were going to throw bags and books in the corner, head for the mountains with flasks and sandwiches, come back to a hamburger joint that evening, and end up with a movie. Once again, each was asked to write down the names of three pupils each would choose to accompany him/her on that trip. These slips of paper were also placed in my briefcase. That night I counted out the 'votes'. All the best students were usually chosen for the project, and all the 'fun-kids' were usually chosen for the day-trip! This gave me a good insight into how they saw each other. What was most helpful, however, was to discover those kids whom nobody had chosen for either undertaking. These were the ones I chose for all the little posts of responsibility in the class! This involved errands, roll books, locking up presses, etc. In no time at all, they had gained a whole new status in the eyes of their peers, and, more especially, in their own eyes.

> *Lord Jesus, you became like me, so that I could become like you. Please reveal that extraordinary fact to my heart, because I have no desire to be able to understand it in my head. Please free me from the petty thinking that would cut you down to my size, and to my way of thinking and acting. I pray that your Spirit may continue to invite me into the fulness of the life of the Trinity. Thanks, Lord, for such an infinite gift. Amen.*

39. Adopted into the family

Scripture speaks of God appearing to his people in many guises. Sometimes in the burning bush, sometimes in the fire by night, the cloud by day, and sometimes in the whispering breeze. After the resurrection, there was some confusion among the followers of Jesus Christ. Mary Magdelene thought he was a gardener, Peter thought he was a ghost, and the disciples on the road to Emmaus thought he was a tourist. Nothing was the same anymore. And that is exactly how it is: nothing is the same anymore. When Jesus ascended into heaven, he brought the body he had with him. From then on, his body is the unit of which each of us is a part. Like parts of a body, each of us is unique and different. A central tenet of Christianity is to see Christ in everybody, and to be Christ to everybody. At first, second, or third glance, that is impossible! There are people I meet and I wonder how God himself can see Christ in them! God never asks me to do something beyond my ability. By myself, I just cannot see Christ in most people. I'm sure my ministry would be relatively easy if I could see Christ in all those to whom I minister. What is supposed to happen is this: I am ready and willing to be Christ to others, and God supplies the Spirit that enables me do that. This can never be perfect, because only God is perfect, but I'm 'marked' on goodwill, and not on perfection. After I make myself available to be Christ to others, an extraordinary thing happens: The Christ in the other begins to reveal himself, and soon I begin to see Christ in that other. It all happens in a gradual progression of revelation, as a whole vista opens up before me. Have you ever heard the phrase: 'She's really very nice when you get to know her'?

I said earlier that at this time on earth, Christ's body is the unit of which each of us is a part. In the gospels Christ's body was glorified, crucified, and resurrected. When I reach out to lift up some person who is broken, is it not a question of the resurrected Christ ministering to the crucified Christ? Christ is in all of us, is working through all of us. To be a Christian it is not possible to have a separate existence outside of Christ. Christ is still being crucified, is still being spat upon, is still being rejected. I can join Mary any day, as she stands at the foot of the cross of many a representative of Christ. Christianity is not some esoteric celluloid cartoon. It is about flesh and blood, about life and death, about good and bad. It involves a whole way of being, a whole way of living. It is something to which we are invited, to which we are called, for which we are chosen. 'You did not choose me, I chose you, and I appointed you to go and bear fruit, and that your fruit would remain.' To see ourselves as extensions of Jesus can help. 'I am the vine, you are the branches. Make sure that you live in me, because, apart from me you have no life.' As a branch, I am part of what the vine is. I have no life apart from the vine. This is full adoption, total belonging, complete identification with the other.

A king had no son to succeed him. He posted a notice inviting young men to come along, and apply for adoption into his family. The two qualifications were love of God, and love of neighbour. A poor peasant boy was tempted to apply, but felt unable to do so because of the rags he wore. He worked hard, earned some money, bought some new clothes, and headed off to try his luck at being adopted into the family of the king.

He was half-way there, however, when he met a poor beggar on the road, who was shivering with the cold. The young man felt sorry for him, and exchanged clothes with him. There was hardly much point in going further towards the king's palace at this stage, now that he was back in rags again. However, the young man felt that, having come this far, he might as well finish the journey.

He arrived at the palace, and, despite the sneers and jibes of the courtiers, he was finally admitted into the presence of the king. Imagine his amazement to see that the king was the old beggar-man he had met on the road, and he was actually wearing the good clothes the young man had given him! The king got down from his throne, embraced the young man, and said, 'Welcome, my son!'

Yes, indeed, Jesus is to be found along the roads of life. Trouble is, it may not be easy to recognise him. One of the priests of my own Congregation, Father Damien the Leper, was beatified over a year ago. This story never fails to inspire and challenge. He became a missioner by default, because his brother was taken ill, and was unable to travel. Damien, although not yet a priest, volunteered to take his place. His arrival among the Lepers on the island of Molokai was a total shock for him. It was the Land that God Forgot, a veritable hell-hole. It was literally a place where the saying held good 'Abandon hope all you who enter here.' For the first few weeks, he couldn't enter the huts of the lepers, because of the stench. He began to smoke a pipe, to try and counteract the smell. With God's help, and God's help only, soon he was washing their sores, and bandaging them. He held them as they died, and he dug their graves. He knew it would be crazy to begin to speak to them of God's love for them! How could he possibly expect them to believe that? So he tried something else. He loved them, and, because of that very fact, they actually came to believe that God loved them. He used light his pipe, take a pull, and pass it around for others to share. He would eat with his hands from the same dish from which others ate, even when they had hands that had no fingers. Like Jesus and us, he became one of them. He contracted leprosy, and died in the prime of life. It is people like him who make the gospel credible. He preached a sermon through his actions, and if his actions didn't speak of gospel values, then his words would be a total sham. 'What you do speaks so loudly, that I cannot hear what you are saying.' The Christian herself is the message. If I have the love of God in my heart, that is what I bring to each situation, even before I open my mouth. Once again, I stress that it is about being an instrument. I supply the hands, feet, and voice, and the Lord supplies the power. The kingdom, the power, and the glory are his.

Heavenly Father, thank you for offering me total adoption into your family. I really do wish to avail fully of that offer. I trust your Spirit to enable me have the attitude necessary, so that your plan may come to completion in me. Please don't let me spoil something so beautiful, by altering it, or cutting it down to my specifications. Amen.

40. Hunger in the midst of plenty

The problem with today's world is not scarcity of food. It fact there is far too much food. The problem is that the food is not available to everybody. Half the world is dying of hunger, and the other half is on a diet, trying to get down the weight! We have butter mountains, and wine lakes, and we are running out of space in which to store the surplus. On occasions, we read of millions of tonnes of wheat being burned or buried, just to ensure that the price remains high. This unequal distribution of wealth, food, and resources is the great obscenity of our time. In the realm of economics, it is very difficult to correct this, because economists are always afraid of creating imbalances, and upsetting national gross production, etc. Once again, this is what happens when people live in their heads. The dreamer who lives in the heart would see a solution, but, then, who would listen? Dreamers have never had huge audiences.

Submitting God to the microscope of my little mind creates serious and imponderable problems. I myself am so limited in every possible way, and God is infinite. When Jesus speaks of life, he speaks of abundant life. He speaks of joy pressed down and flowing over. It is his peace that he offers. This peace is endless and eternal, and it is something totally different from just the absence of war. St Augustine speaks of watching a young lad on a beach. He had made a hole in the sand. He had a small bucket, and he went back and forth from the water's edge to the hole, carrying buckets of water. When asked what he was doing, he replied that he intended pouring the sea into the hole in the sand! Ridiculous, no doubt, but a very good analogy for the situation when I try to contain God in my understanding, or in my consciousness. I can think only in finites, and God is infinite. That's what Thomas Aquinas means when he says that whatever I say about God, I can be sure of only one thing: I'll be wrong! God is so much more than anything I could possibly conceive of, or imagine. Because, looking at God from my perspective, I am totally limited and handicapped, I have to trust that God himself will reveal his view-point of things. Jesus certainly couldn't give any more than he did. 'I asked my God how much he loved me, and he stretched out his arms fully to either side, and said. "This much", and then he died.' Jesus uses the term 'banquet' a great deal, when he speaks of the invitation of the Father. He is doing everything possible to impress upon us the idea of prodigal generosity. His love has no end. 'So high you can't get over it, so low, you can't get under it, so wide, you can't get around it, love, wonderful love.'

Like most other people, I, too, often try to fantasise what this present life will look like when I pass on to the third and final stage. Obviously, I don't know, but I cannot help thinking that it was awash with gift and grace in prodigal abundance, and, for some reason, I settled for a subsistence level of that life. The 'some reason' is probably my tendency to keep God within the confines of my own finite capacity for being. Ideally, I think of the ageing process as the body growing smaller, and more limited, and the inner person becoming much larger, more expansive, and much much more tolerant. I think if the process doesn't do that, then it is a great pity that it lasted this length, because it would seem to be a great waste. I remember an old man living on his own in a southern town in Ireland. An old beggarman often used the front window-sill of this man's house, where he could sit, rest, beg, and chat with the passers-by. The old man of the house had no objections to this, and they were reasonably well acquainted. Anyhow, the old man wasn't seen around for a few days, and when the police entered his house, they found him dead in bed, from natural causes. What surprised everybody was the huge amount of cash the police found stashed away in biscuit tins all over the house. Poor old Mike, who spent hours every day sitting on the front window-sill, used joke that he had been sitting on a veritable gold-mine all those times, and he never knew it!

The New York Times carried a story some years ago, about a 90-year-old widow, who was found, close to starvation, in a run-down, rat-infested apartment. She had been well-known in the neighbourhood as someone who was always to be seen rummaging in garbage cans for scraps, or collecting cardboard and bits of sticks for the miserly fire she occasionally lit in the winter. She lived on hot dogs.

Three weeks later, the woman died in a New York hospital. When they cleaned her apartment they found $275,000 in paper money, stashed away in cardboard boxes.

When I was growing up, I thought we were poor, because my parents didn't have a lot of money. It was years later when I came to discover just how rich we were. The woman in this story had a lot of money, but she was very poor indeed. It is a frightening thing when, instead of possessing something, that thing begins to possess me. It can be that way with money. 'Freedom's just another word for nothing left to lose.' I am not at all suggesting that we don't need money! There comes a time, however, when there is an obvious distinction between what I need and what I want. They say that, for the alcoholic, there's never enough alcohol. No matter how much you give me today, I'll still want more to-morrow. It can become like that with money. For some people there's never enough. They are always chasing the rainbow. They know the price of everything and the value of nothing. They worship the idol of wealth, and it becomes a tyrant.

I referred earlier to what it might possibly look like as I look back at life from the next stage. The woman in our story could be more real than I now realise. It is just possible that she did not honestly appreciate what she had after a while. Her mind still acted as it did when she had nothing. Collecting and saving money became an end in itself. She might never actually have thought of spending any of it. She may have needed the sense of owning rather than the joy of spending. For me, now, I could live in turmoil, guilt, worry, and discouragement, even if I possess a fountain of living water within my soul. I heard that I had, but it may not have dawned on me to make use of it, to turn to it in my aridity, and to be open to a whole new spring. It is like dying of thirst in a brewery, if I may be forgiven the analogy! God makes his graces, his gifts, and his blessings available to me, but he sure ain't going to force them on me. He offers me peace, but I'm totally free to live in misery and die of ulcers if I want to!

Education is about going from the known to the unknown. When it comes to God's love, the only love we really know is human love. This is our point of origin. If we could multiply this by infinity and make it last for eternity, we would have some idea. If we take the most unconditional love we've ever known, and multiply that by the number of people in the whole world, we begin to expand our understanding towards more realistic proportions, which, however, will still be infinitely short of the scope of God's love. And who says we're not sitting on a gold-mine?!

Holy Spirit, Breath of God, you are the Power, the Love, and the Life of the Trinity. You have made your home in my heart. Please, please reveal to my spirit the wonders of this truth. Fill me with joy, praise, and gratitude for the extraordinary privilege that is mine. Please continue to remind me, especially when I tend to forget, that even God could not do any more than what He is making available to me right now. Thank you, Lord. Amen.

Thematic Index

Numbers refer to story numbers

Attitude 23, 34, 35, 38, 39.
Baptism 20.
Children 3, 5, 6, 7, 14, 15, 16, 17, 19, 21, 22, 23, 24, 25, 35, 38.
Christian 7, 8, 13, 14, 20, 24, 25, 27, 32, 38.
Christmas 23.
Community 8, 14, 27.
Conversion 11, 15, 16, 24, 30, 38, 40.
Death 5, 6, 9, 10, 12, 19, 21, 40.
Decision 15, 16, 30, 31, 33, 35, 38.
Despair 5, 7, 13, 38.
Example 3, 23, 35, 38.
Faith 5, 10, 20, 21.
Family 14, 19, 21, 23, 25, 35, 38.
Father's Love 5, 17, 18, 21, 23, 28, 35, 39.
Forgiveness 26.
Gift 18, 23.
Heart 6, 8, 16, 34, 38.
Heaven 1, 4, 5, 6, 11, 17.
Hell 4, 11.
Holy Spirit 2, 24.
Hope 6, 20, 26, 39.
Jesus 2, 3, 29, 36.
Lies 15, 16, 38.
Love 4, 19, 21, 23, 28, 36, 37.
Marriage 37.
Mothers 20, 21, 25.
Religion 1, 8, 22, 31.
Saint 25, 26.
Salvation 1, 18, 29, 32.
Satan 20.
Service 8, 9, 36.
Sin 15, 16, 26, 32, 40.
Trust 7, 10, 21.
Truth 16, 32, 38.
World 33, 34.